The Ama

An Exploration Of Countries, Cultures, And Creatures

A Learning Center
For
Secondary School Students

Conceived and Developed

By

James L. Castner

The Amazon Rainforest

An Exploration Of Countries, Cultures, And Creatures

A Learning Center For Secondary School Students

By: James Lee Castner

Published by:

> Feline Press
> P.O. Box 357219
> Gainesville, FL
> 32635   USA

All rights reserved. No part of this book may be reproduced or transmitted in any form or by any means, electronic or mechanical, including photocopying, recording, or by any information storage and retrieval system currently known or yet to be developed, without written permission from the publisher, except for the inclusion of brief quotations in a review, or unless specifically labeled as a reproducible page.

© 1999 by Feline Press, Inc.
First Printing 1999
Printed in Canada

ISBN 0-9625150-9-4

Library of Congress
Catalog Card Number:
98-94792

Acknowledgments

I would like to thank John Jenkins who encouraged me to develop this work as a resource that could be published and used by teachers throughout the country. I thank Kathy Shewey for introducing me to the subject of learning centers and for making many of her own personal reference materials available to me. I would like to thank Paul George and Kathy Shewey for their instruction in the graduate course The Emergent Middle School, and for opening my eyes to the world of middle school children.

I would also like to thank the following people for having taken time from their busy schedules to read the manuscript and provide me with many useful suggestions and comments: Jim Cronk, Paul George, John Jenkins, Bruce Kemlitz, Bill Lorowitz, Steve Madigosky, Jan Propst, Andra Raboin, Bruce Rinker, Kathy Shewey, Stephen Timme, and Janet Wisby. I would especially like to thank Jan Propst for her interaction on the *Arts and Artifacts* and *Music and Dance* sections. Much of the former section was derived from her own curriculum unit titled *Amazon Artisans: An Interdisciplinary Discovery Of Amazon Rain Forest Culture.*

Some of my classmates worked on projects which also stimulated various ideas or which provided information in the form of references and resources. I would like to thank them for providing me with copies of their class projects: Lawson Brown, Angela Cascio, Debora Craig, Pam Kellie Knapp, Carol Lowe, Brad McLeland, Lindsey Myers, Karen Pickett, and Rose Simpson.

During the course of researching this work I spent much time in the pleasant atmosphere of the Book Gallery West in Gainesville, FL. My thanks to the owner and helpful staff who allowed me to use their computer and data bases. I would also like to thank the staff of Kanapaha Middle School in Gainesville, who permitted me to invade their Media Center and photograph my learning stations. Final thanks to all my rainforest workshop colleagues and friends. Thanks for all the good times.

Dedication

I would like to dedicate this work to Juanita, an educator who represents all that is good and worthwhile in teaching. Her love for her students and dedication to her career and family is an inspiration to all.

James

Sample Learning Station

A learning station that has the central display made of photographs mounted on a three-section 'science board'. The display catches the eye and piques student interest, while additional information and materials are provided close by. This display can fold flat for storage.

Foreword

For veteran rainforest enthusiasts or for teachers and students embarking on their first adventure of tropical forest and cultural studies, Castner's learning center provides a wealth of varied background information with learning purpose, direction and outcomes clearly defined.

Written for the middle school audience (though adaptable to upper elementary and high school settings), a number of Castner's suggested learning activities would demand upper level competencies from fairly self-directed students if used strictly as a stand-alone learning center.

As a former 6th grade teacher, I could see an extended, multi-disciplinary thematic unit being developed utilizing the information and guidelines presented. Combined with pre- and post-assessments, many of the suggested learning activities are ideally suited for the hands-on, personal and experiential involvements which typify middle level delivery strategies and learning styles. Utilizing Castner's learning center, including his wonderfully researched list of teaching resources, motivated students working in teams or cooperative groups, along with teachers guiding them, will find no end to the diversity of Amazon discoveries waiting for them!

To have such a middle level teaching and learning resource designed by a veteran rainforest scientist, one who has dedicated much of his life to researching and teaching about this diverse and most crucial of ecosystems, is indeed a rare treat!

Jim Cronk, former 6th Grade Teacher
Zeeland Middle School (Zeeland, Michigan)
Co-founder and Board Chairman
Children's Environmental Trust Foundation, International

Table of Contents

Learning Stations

Additional Materials and Information

Introduction

Learning centers have gained wide acceptance at the middle and high school levels by providing a great deal of instructional variety and flexibility to both the teacher and the student. Such centers are often used in conjunction with the teaching of a unifying theme or unit. Their complexity and depth into a particular subject, or aspect of a subject, is only limited by the creativity of the designer. This learning center presents a group of ten individual learning stations, each of which deals with a particular aspect or topic relating to the Amazon Rainforest and/or South America.

A learning center by definition is an area in the classroom which contains a collection of activities and materials to teach, reinforce, and enrich a skill or concept (Schurr 1995). Part of the appeal is that they function well for students who vary in abilities, and especially for those students who are active and self-directed learners. In the latter case, self-direction skills are developed through the selection of which learning stations to complete and deciding which activities to do within a station. Physical movement is an integral part of any multi-station learning center and is an appropriate consideration for middle school-age students.

Each station should present activities and information in a variety of ways that correspond to the different ways in which students learn. Not all individuals learn with equal ease from the same instructional methods. Thus, the greater the variety of activities and presentation of information, the greater the chance that all students participating will be reached and benefit from this information. With this in mind, I have presented a number of ideas for catching student interest and engaging their minds on a topic about which I feel passionately (the rainforest). Activities span a range of difficulty levels and have been conceived to serve all types of learners (visual, audial, active, and writing-oriented). The beauty of such learning centers is that any teacher can modify, combine, or completely change them to suit their own personal set of teaching circumstances. The information presented here has the purpose of serving as a starting point or springboard. It should prove useful to any educator interested in pursuing the topics of rainforests, the Amazon, South America, or Latin culture in conjunction with their curriculum.

This learning center contains ten separate stations. Each station is presented in the context of the following organizational outline: **Rationale, Prior-Knowledge Questions, Answers To Prior-Knowledge Questions, Objectives, Activities, Assessment, Materials,** and **Resources**. The Rationales have been written to the teachers. They may be used as an Introduction or teachers may wish to write their own Rationales for each topic directed specifically to their students. An example of such a 'student-oriented' Rationale has been included at the end of the book with the Reproducible Pages (see page 92). The Reproducible Pages contain information that serves as an introduction to each topic, and may be photocopied and used as part of each station.

My concept of the use of the Prior-Knowledge Questions is for teachers to determine whether or not some students are already sufficiently knowledgeable on a particular topic, thus permitting them to skip the corresponding learning station and its activities. If the Prior-Knowledge Questions for all the learning stations are given at one time before this unit or learning center is started, teachers will be able to pinpoint specific areas of strengths and weaknesses. Answers such as "I don't know" are acceptable, since they provide the needed information. The Answers To Prior-Knowledge Questions section provides educators with a guide for evaluating student responses.

The remaining sections of each station are self-explanatory and can be changed or modified to suit individual instructors' needs. They are included to serve as a guide and starting point. Often the items listed in the Activities and the Assessment sections are interchangeable. I have been especially thorough in the Resources sections, to make it easy for teachers to locate and obtain functional materials. Some of the resources are advanced level materials meant only to serve for teacher reference, while others are obviously for student use.

The physical components of the individual stations will be selected or created by the teachers, limited only by space, resources, and creativity. Three-sided panels of 'foam core' (sometimes called 'science boards', see page *iv*) are an excellent medium for display since they are lightweight and can be folded for near flat storage if designed with that in mind. Simple cardboard or foam core carrols can be constructed to add a degree of privacy for students working in a multi-use area. A strategy to help ensure success is to have students help with the construction and design of appropriate physical and visual components of each station. Class projects could even revolve around the development of such a center.

6

References

Dynamite In The Classroom - A How to Handbook For Teachers
Sandra L. Schurr
National Middle School Association   Columbus, OH
1989   ISBN 1-56090-041-5

Multiple Intelligences Activities (Grades 5-8)
Julia Jasmine
Teacher Created Materials   Huntington Beach, CA
1996   ISBN 1-55734-399-3

Prescription For Success In Heterogenous Classrooms
Sandra L. Schurr
National Middle School Association   Columbus, OH
1995   ISBN 1-56090-097-0

Cooperative Learning Activities In The Library Media Center
Lesley J. Farmer
Libraries Unlimited, Inc.   Englewood, CO
Phone: 1-800-237-6124

Secondary Learning Centers
An Innovative Approach To Individualized Instruction
Clifford P. Bee
Goodyear Publishing Co.   Santa Monica, CA
1980   ISBN: 0-8302-8203-3

Teaching Secondary School Students Through Their Individual
*   Learning Styles - Practical Approaches For Grades 7-12*
Rita S. Dunn and Kenneth J. Dunn
Allyn & Bacon, Inc.   Needham Heights, MA
1993   ISBN: 0-2051-3308-8

Learning Style Profile Handbook
II. Accomodating Perceptual, Study and Instructional Preferences
James W. Keefe
National Association Of Secondary School Principals (NASSP)
1989   Reston, VA

Companies And Organizations
With Products For Teachers

National Middle School Association
2600 Corporate Exchange Drive, Suite 370
Columbus, OH 43231-1672
Phone: (800)-528-NMSA

National Geographic Educational Catalog
1145 17th Street, N.W.
Washington, D.C. 20036-4688
Phone: (800)-368-2728

World Book Educational Products
Phone: (800)-WORLD BK
Phone: (800)-726-0600

National Science Teachers Association
1840 Wilson Boulevard
Arlington, VA 22201-3000
Phone: (703)-243-7100

Teacher Ideas Press
Dept. G, P.O. Box 6633
Englewood, CO 80155-6633
Phone: (800)-237-6124

Instructional Fair - TS Denison
Pre-K Through High School
P.O. Box 1650
Grand Rapids, MI 49501
Phone: (800)-443-2976

Feline Press
P.O. Box 357219
Gainesville, FL 32635
Phone: (352)-371-6439
e-mail: JLCASTNER@AOL.COM

Frank Schaffer Publications
P.O. Box 60950
Los Angeles, CA 90060-0950
Phone: (800)-421-5533

Carson-Dellosa
P.O. Drawer 35665
Greensboro, N.C. 27425-5665
Phone: (800)-321-0943

Trend Enterprises
P.O. Box 64073
St. Paul. MN 55164
Phone: (800)-328-0818

Teacher Created Materials, Inc.
P.O. Box 1040
Huntington Beach, CA 92647
Phone: (800)-858-7339

Evan Moor Corporation
18 Lower Ragsdale Drive
Monterey, CA 93940-5746
Phone: (800)-777-4489

Learning Resources
380 N. Fairway Drive
Vernon Hills, IL 60061
Phone: (800)-222-3909

Educational Insights
16941 Keegan Avenue
Carson, CA 90746
Phone: (800)-995-4436

Creative Teaching Press
10701 Holder Street
Cypress, CA 90630-0017
Phone: (800)-444-4287

Learning Station One

Welcome to South America!
¡Bienvenidos a Sud America!

Rationale

This will be the first stop for the students, while the other learning stations may be completed in any order. It is an appropriate place to have sheets of printed questions available in order to determine the extent of knowledge that already exists in the class. The questions for such an assessment can come from the Prior-Knowledge Questions presented in the following learning stations. The results of these 'tests' may indicate that some students are already knowledgeable in certain areas and can skip specific stations.

The introductory station is unique in that it does not conform to the organizational outline followed in all other learning stations. It functions as a blueprint and guide, allowing students to see at a glance what subjects and themes will be in store for them at the other stations throughout the center. In addition to an assessment of exisiting knowledge, a statement of general directions, rules of usage, and a schedule of hours for classes using the center can be posted.

The ways in which this particular learning station can be created are limitless, but it should be remembered that this may be the students' first exposure to the theme of the Amazon Rainforest and South America. Bearing this in mind, teachers should make every effort to actively engage students and convince them that completing this learning center will be enjoyable as well as educational. The use of visual aids in the form of colorful, eye-catching photographs or posters is one way to attract attention. There is certainly a wealth of such materials available, both commercially and from conservation organizations (see pages 17-20). Use of materials from the latter will familiarize students with the names of some of the organizations that are trying to stem rainforest destruction. Photographs provided by teachers who have traveled to South America will identify certain faculty members as possible adult 'experts' to be interviewed by students and to give presentations.

It is also possible that some of the students in the class have traveled to a rainforest or even lived in South America. A suggestion is to mount a large map of South America at this station that the students can examine. Near it should be a banner with the question: "Where in South America have you been?" Push-pins and slips of paper should be provided so that students can write their names on the slips and pin them to the appropriate location they've visited. This will permit the entire class to know who has traveled to locations throughout South America, and it shall identify which students will potentially be able to serve in the capacity as 'peer experts' with a source of firsthand knowledge and experience.

Unusual objects and artifacts are another way to attract the students' attention. I suggest that you put out one item or one photo that represents each learning station, along with an engaging or teasing caption that might appeal to secondary school humor. For example, a photo of Indians using a blowgun in conjunction with a caption that reads: "Have you ever used a blowgun? If you want to learn more about it, visit the Arts and Artifacts Learning Station." Another example would be to have the container available from a medicine that is derived from a rainforest plant. The legend might read: "Do you know what rainforest plant was used to make this medicine? If not, visit the Plants for People Learning Station." Following this lead, something should be presented that will attract students to each of the learning stations that make up the center.

Materials

Bulletin board, map of South America, push-pins, slips of paper, pen/pencil, books, posters, postcards, photographs, artifacts.

Resources

Books

South America - A Homework Booklet   (Juvenile)
Harriet Kinghorn, Helen Colella, and Diane Fusaro
Instructional Fair, Inc.   Grand Rapids, MI
1996   ISBN 1-56822-189-4

A Unit About Tropical Rainforests   (Juvenile)
Debby DePauw
Evan-Moor Corp.   Monterey, CA
1993   ISBN 1-55799-276-2

Using The Internet To Explore Rain Forests (Juvenile)
Jan Nutt
Steck-Vaughn Co.   Austin, TX
1997   ISBN 0-8172-6787-5

Rain Forests   (Juvenile)
Theresa Greenaway
Dorling Kindersley Ltd.   London
1994   ISBN 0-679-86168-8

The Rain Forest   (Juvenile)
Billy Goodman
Tern Enterprise, Inc.   New York, N.Y.
1991   ISBN 0-316-32019-6

Rain Forests   (Juvenile)
Joy Palmer
Steck-Vaughn Co.   Austin, TX
1993   ISBN 0-8114-3400-1

Exotic Rainforests   (Juvenile)
Anita Ganeri
A Golden Book   New York, N.Y.
1992   ISBN 0-307-15606-0

The Amazon   (Juvenile)
M. Pollard
Marshall Cavendish   Tarrytown, N.Y.
1998   ISBN 0-7614-0501-1

Tropical Rainforest   (Juvenile)
Michael Bright
Franklin Watts   New York, N.Y.
1991   ISBN 0-531-17301-1

Books (cont.)

The Great Kapok Tree   (Juvenile)
Lynne Cherry
Harcourt Brace Jovanovich   San Diego, CA
1990   ISBN 0-15-200520-X

A Walk In The Rainforest   (Juvenile)
Kristin Joy Pratt
DAWN Publications   Nevada City, CA
1992   ISBN 1-878265-53-9

Learn About Rainforests   (Juvenile)
Jen Green
Lorenz Books   New York, N.Y.
1998   ISBN 1-85967-759-2

Tropical Rain Forests   (Juvenile)
Emilie U. Lepthien
Children's Press
Grolier Publishing   Danbury, CT
1993   ISBN 0-516-01198-7

Rainforests   (Juvenile)
Edward R. Ricciuti
Marshall Cavendish   Tarrytown, N.Y.
1996   ISBN 0-7614-0078-8

Nature's Green Umbrella
Tropical Rain Forests   (Juvenile)
Gail Gibbons
Morrow Junior Books   New York, N.Y.
1994   ISBN 0-688-12353-8

Tropical Rain Forests Of Central America (Juvenile)
Alberto De Larramendi Ruis
Children's Press
Grolier Publishing   Danbury, CT
1993   ISBN 0-516-08383-X

The Amazon Rainforest
An Exploration Of Countries, Cultures, And Creatures
A Learning Center For Secondary School Students
James L. Castner
Feline Press   Gainesville, FL
1999   ISBN 0-9625150-9-4

In The Rainforest
Catherine Caufield
U. of Chicago Press   New York, N.Y.
1984   ISBN 0-226-09786-2

The Rainforests - A Celebration
Lisa Silcock (Editor)
Chronicle Books   San Francisco, CA
1989   ISBN 0-8118-0155-1

Portraits Of The Rainforest
Adrian Forsyth
Firefly Books   Ontario, Canada
1990   ISBN 0-921820-13-5

Vanishing Paradise - The Tropical Rainforest
Andrew Mitchell
Overlook Press   Woodstock, N.Y.
1990   ISBN 0-87951-406-X

Rainforests
Norman Myers
Rodale Press   Emmaus, PA
1993   ISBN 0-87596-597-0

The Rainforest
D'Arcy Richardson
Smithmark Publishers, Inc.   New York, N.Y.
1991   ISBN 0-8317-7342-1

Books (cont.)

Tropical Nature
Adrian Forsyth and Ken Miyata
Charles Scribner's Sons New York, N.Y.
1987 ISBN 0-684-18710-8

A Neotropical Companion
John C. Kricher
Princeton University Press Princeton, N.J.
1989 ISBN 0-691-08521-8

Rainforests
James L. Castner
Feline Press Gainesville, FL
1990 ISBN 0-9625150-2-7

A Parrot Without A Name
Don Stap
University of Texas Press Austin, TX
1990 ISBN 0-292-76529-0

Jungles
Edward Ayensu (Editor)
Crown Publishers New York, N.Y.
1980 ISBN 0-517-54136-X

Amazonia
Loren McIntyre
Sierra Club Books San Francisco, CA
1991 ISBN 0-87156-641-9

Out Of The Amazon
Sue Cunningham and Ghillean T. Prance
HMSO Publications London, U.K.
1992 ISBN 0-11-250074-9

Tropical Rainforest
Arnold Newman
Facts On File New York, N.Y.
1990 ISBN 0-8160-1944-4

Four Neotropical Rainforests
Alwyn H. Gentry (Editor)
Yale University Press   New Haven, CT
1990   ISBN 0-300-05448-3

Inside The Amazing Amazon
Don Lessem
Crown Publishers   New York, N.Y.
1995   ISBN 0-517-59490-0

Rainforests Of The World
Ghillean T. Prance
Crown Publishers   New York, N.Y.
1998   ISBN 0-609-60364-7

The Tropical Rain Forest
Marius Jacobs
Springer-Verlag   Berlin, Germany
1981   ISBN 3-540-17996-8

La Selva
Lucinda A. McDade and others (Editors)
U. of Chicago Press   Chicago, IL
1994   ISBN 0-226-03952-8

The Ecology Of A Tropical Forest
Egbert G. Leigh, Jr. and others (Editors)
Smithsonian Institution Press Washington, D.C.
1982   ISBN 0-87474-601-9

Magazine Articles
Amazon Issue
Kids Discover
October 1996   Vol. 6, Issue 8

Rain Forests Issue
Kids Discover
Phone: (212)-242-5133

Videos
Jungle
1994   PBS Video
Phone: (800)-645-4727

Web Of Life: Exploring Biodiversity
QED Communications
1995   Pittsburg, PA
Phone: (800)-274-1307

Exploring The Diversity Of Life
Environmental Media Corporation
1997   Chapel Hill, N.C.
Phone: (800)-368-3382

Rain Forest
National Geographic Society
1983   Washington, D.C.
Phone: (800)-627-5162

Heroes Of The High Frontier
National Geographic Society
1999   Washington, D.C.
Phone: (800)-627-5162

Tropical Rainforest
IMAX (check the Internet for the nearest IMAX theater)

Rain Forest, *Selva Verde*, and *Spirits Of The Forest*
Nature Series

Journey To A Thousand Rivers, *The New Eldorado*, *Snowstorm In
     The Jungle*, and *Invaders And Exiles*
The Cousteau Collection

Creatures Of The Amazon
Best of Bill Burrud Collection

Organizations within the United States

Bat Conservation International
P.O. Box 162603
Austin, TX 78716
Phone: (512)-327-9721

Children's Environmental Trust Foundation, International
627 Central Avenue East
Zeeland, MI 49464
Phone: (888)-748-9993

Conservation International
1015 18th Street, NW
Suite 1002
Washington, D.C. 20036
Phone: (202)-429-5660

Cultural Survival
96 Mount Auburn Street
Cambridge, MA 02138
Phone: (617)-441-5400

Earthwatch
680 Mount Auburn Street
P.O. Box 9104
Watertown, MA 02272-9104
Phone: (617)-926-8200

Environmental Defense Fund
257 Park Avenue South
New York, N.Y. 10010
Phone: (212)-505-2100

Friends Of The Earth
1025 Vermont Avenue, NW
Suite 300
Washington, D.C. 20005-6303
Phone: (202)-783-7400

Organizations within the United States (cont.)

Greenpeace
Tropical Forests Campaign
1436 U Street, NW
No. 201-A
Washington, D.C. 20009
Phone: (202)-462-8817

The International Canopy Network (ICAN)
2103 Harrison Avenue, NW
Suite 2612
Olympia, WA 98502-2607
Phone: (360)-866-6788

JASON Foundation for Education
395 Totten Pond Road
Waltham, MA 02451
Phone: (781)-487-9995

National Wildlife Federation
1400 16th Street, NW
Suite 501
Washington, D.C. 20036
Phone: (202)-797-6800

Nature Conservancy
International Program
1785 Massachusetts Avenue, NW
Washington, D.C. 20036
Phone: (202)-488-0231

Organization For Tropical Studies (O.T.S.)
Box 90632
Durham, N.C. 27708-0632
Phone: (919)-684-5774

Rainforest Action Network
301 Broadway
Suite A
San Francisco, CA 94133
Phone: (415)-398-4404

Rainforest Alliance
65 Bleecker Street
New York, N.Y. 10012-2420
Phone: (212)-677-1900

The School For Field Studies
16 Broadway
Beverly, MA 01915-4499
Phone: (508)-927-7777

Summer Institute of Linguistics (SIL)
International Academic Bookstore
7500 West Camp Wisdom Road
Dallas, TX 75236-5626
Phone: (214)-709-2404

U.S. Fish and Wildlife Service
Department of the Interior
18th and C Streets, NW
Washington, D.C. 20240

World Resources Institute
1709 New York Avenue, NW
Washington, D.C. 2006
Phone: (800)-822-0504

World Wildlife Fund
1250 24th Street, NW
Washington, D.C. 20037
Phone: (202)-293-4800

Organizations outside the United States

Friends Of The Earth
Fourth Floor
56 Foster Street
Surrey Hills
NSW 2010, Australia

Gaia Foundation
18 Well Walk
Hampstead, London
NW3 1LD, England
Phone: (44-171)-431-5000

Living Earth
10 Upper Grosvenor Street
London
W1X 9PA, England

Rainforest Foundation
5 Fitzroy Lodge, The Grove
Highgate, London
N6 5JU, England

Survival International
310 Edgware Road
London
W2 1DY, England

United Nations Educational Scientific And Cultural Organization (UNESCO)
7, Place de Fontenoy, F-75007
Paris, France
Phone: 33-(1)-45-68-1000

World Wildlife Fund International
Avenue du Mont-Blanc
1196 Gland
Switzerland

Geography of South America
Where in the world?

Rationale

The Amazon rainforest is often mentally associated with Brazil. Although much of this rainforest is located within Brazil, the entire Amazon River Basin and its tropical forest extends into many other countries. A clear understanding of South American geography will not only help students to visualize spatially where the places under discussion exist, but can also be used to tie in the exploration and colonization of the South American continent by various world powers. This learning station will also facilitate student comprehension of regional and cultural differences and the reasons why they exist.

Prior-Knowledge Questions

1. How many countries are there in South America? Name them and their capitals, if you can. Which is the largest? The smallest?
2. Draw a rough map of North America, Central America, and South America. Indicate the equator and the Panama Canal.
3. Are any countries in South America landlocked? Which?
4. Which countries does the Amazon River run through?
5. Which countries have areas of tropical forest?
6. What large rivers besides the Amazon are found in South America?
7. How big is the Amazon Basin compared to the United States?
8. What is the average annual rainfall in the Amazon rainforest?
9. What is the approximate length of the Amazon River?
10. How much water flows through the Amazon River in comparison to the Mississippi? (The same? Twice as much? More?)
11. What portion of the world's rainforests does the Amazon make up?
12. What mountain chain extends north-south through South America?
13. Where is the driest area of South America?
14. Which South American countries does the equator pass through?
15. What is the highest waterfall in the world and what country is it in?
16. What is the highest mountain in South America?

17. What is the name of the cold water current that flows off the west coast of South America? After what person is it named? What did this person do?

18. What is the latitiude of your school? What countries does that same latitude fall through in South America? If the latitude is the same, are these countries experiencing the same weather or season as you right now? If you answered no, explain why not. What factors other than latitude might affect the climate of a particular place?

19. What are *tepuis* and where are they found?

Answers to Prior-Knowledge Questions

1. Thirteen. Countries and capitals from biggest to smallest are: Brazil/Brasilia, Argentina/Buenos Aires, Peru/Lima, Colombia/Bogota, Bolivia/La Paz, Venezuela/Caracas, Chile/Santiago, Paraguay/Asuncion, Ecuador/Quito, Guyana/Georgetown, Uruguay/Montevideo, Surinam/Paramaribo, French Guiana/Cayenne.

3. Yes. Bolivia and Paraguay.

4. Major rivers that are tributaries of the Amazon flow through many of the countries of northern South America. However, the name Amazon is only used in Peru and Brazil.

5. Areas of tropical forest are found in Peru, Ecuador, Colombia, Venezuela, Bolivia, Brazil, Guyana, Surinam, and French Guiana.

6. Some are the Orinoco, Napo, Paraná, Ucayali, Marañon, Xingu, Madeira, and Putumayo.

7. The Amazon Basin is about the same size as the continental U.S.

8. The average annual rainfall in the Amazon rainforest is approximately 254 centimeters (100 inches).

9. The Amazon River is approximately 6,720 km (4,000 miles) long.

10. Eleven times as much water flows through the Amazon River.

11. The Amazon rainforest makes up one-third of the world's total.

12. The Andes Mountains.

13. The driest area of South America is desert along the western coast.

14. The equator passes through Ecuador, Colombia, and Brazil.

15. Angel Falls in Venezuela.

16. Mt. Aconcagua in Argentina.

17. The name of the current is the Humboldt Current, after Alexander von Humboldt, a famous explorer and naturalist. In 1800, Humboldt made an extensive journey and studied the geography and wildlife of the Orinoco River Valley.

18. Since it is assumed that the school is in the Northern Hemisphere, seasons would be reversed in the Southern Hemisphere. Another factor that might affect climate is the elevation.
19. Ancient mountainous outcroppings near the border of Brazil, Venezuela, and Guyana.

Objectives

1. Students will be able to name each country of South America, identify it on an outline map, and name and locate its capital.
2. Students will be able to demonstrate that they know the relative size of the countries of South America with respect to one another.
3. Students will be able to locate and identify the major geographical features of the continent (lakes, mountains, rivers, forests, deserts).
4. Students will be able to demonstrate a knowledge of geological history and how it has affected the evolution of animal and plant species in South America.
5. Students will be able to demonstrate a knowledge of weather patterns and their origin based on the geographical features of the South American continent.
6. Students will be able to define/discuss 'ice age' and 'refugia'.

Assessment

(Students are provided with a blank outline map of South America.)
1. Identify on the map each of the countries, and name and place its capital in the approximate location.
2. Make a list of South American countries in decreasing order according to size.
3. Locate (approximately) on the map the major geographical features of the continent including mountains, rivers, forests, and deserts.
4. How has the geological history of South America affected the evolution of its plants and animals? Include in your answer a discussion of plate tectonics, continental drift, and the paleo-continent Gondwanaland.
5. How do the geographical features of South America influence the climate and forest types that we see from the western coast to the Amazon Basin? Include in your answer mention of ocean currents, mountain ranges, and wind currents.
6. Compare and contrast the Mississippi River system of the United States with the Amazon River system of South America.

7. If the equator were shifted 10 degrees of latitude to the south, how would it affect the distribution of rainforests over time? What other effects could be expected from such an event?

8. Use all your knowledge to devise a system of classifying rainforests. You may base your classification scheme on any legitimate criteria you select.

9. Compare and contrast a tropical rainforest from the Amazon Basin with a temperate rainforest in the northwest United States.

10. Define what is meant by Pleistocene refugia or Quarternary refugia. Include mention of 'ice ages' and their causes.

Activities

1. Take a piece of tracing paper and trace the outline of one South American country. Indicate the location of its capital. Compare this country to a map of the United States that is of the same scale. Give the country's approximate size in units equivalent to U.S. states (ex. Country A equals the size of North Carolina and South Carolina together.) Use the atlas or map available to determine the country's actual size and write it down. Fill in all the geographical features on your country. Do this for each of the countries of South America.

2. Take scissors and cut out each of the countries from the tracing paper. Try to identify the countries based on their shape. Place the cut out countries on top of one another in an effort to determine how they relate to one another with respect to size. Check your guesses with the actual area that you wrote down in the previous exercise. Use the separate cut out countries like the pieces of a jigsaw puzzle and try to reconstruct the continent of South America.

3. Make a three-dimensional map, using the materials of your choice, that shows the major geographical features of South America.

4. Observe a world map. Pretend you are going to cut out each continent separately and piece them together as one. How would they all fit?

5. Compare a temperate and tropical rainforest with regards to species richness, rainfall, and temperature.

6. Write a brief report on Leslie R. Holdridge. Include an explanation and definition of a Holdridge Life Zone.

Materials

Atlas, maps, tracing paper, pen/pencil, scissors, and plaster of paris (and/or other map-making materials).

Resources

Maps
Map Link
30 South La Patera Lane
Unit #5
Santa Barbara, CA 93117
Phone: (805)-692-6777

OMNI Resources
1004 South Mebane Street
P.O. Box 2096
Burlington, N.C. 27216-2096
Phone: (800)-742-2677

Central Intelligence Agency
Public Affairs Office
Washington, D.C. 20505
Phone: (803)-351-2053

Facts On File
460 Park Avenue South
New York, N.Y. 10016
Phone: (800)-332-8755

Books
World Geography Series South America   (Juvenile)
Julia Jasmine
Teacher Created Materials   Huntington Beach, CA
1995   ISBN 1-55734-694-1

The Amazon - Time-Life Books
Tom Sterling
Time-Life Intl.   Amsterdam, Holland
1973

Brazil - Life World Library
Elizabeth Bishop
Time Inc.   New York, N.Y.
1962

Colombia And Venezuela And The Guianas - Life World Library
Gary MacEoin
Time Inc.   New York, N.Y.
1965

The Andes - Time-Life Books
Tony Morrison
Time-Life Intl.   Amsterdam, Holland
1976

Organizations
South American Explorers Club
126 Indian Creek Road
Ithaca, N.Y. 14850
Phone: (607)-277-0488

National Geographic Society
1145 17th Street, NW
Washington, D.C. 20036-4688
Phone: (800)-NGS-LINE

The Explorers Club
46 East 70th Street
New York, N.Y. 10021
Phone: (212)-628-8383

Royal Geographical Society
1 Kensington Gore
London
SW7 2AR
England
Phone: (44-171)-589-5466

Biodiversity
Rainforest Flora and Fauna

Rationale

The Amazon Basin houses the greatest diversity of plant and animal species in the world. Just as physical and spatial concepts are difficult to perceive without comparing them to more familiar 'landmarks', so is the concept of biological diversity. One of the guiding themes of this learning center is diversity, a concept that can be easily and excitingly demonstrated with examples from the natural world. A great part of the value that tropical forests hold for humankind is the potential usefulness of all the biological organisms that have yet to be discovered or studied in depth. Many of these are endemic organisms that are only found in a very specific locale and nowhere else. This learning station will expose students to some of the integral components of the natural world that make up the rainforest community.

Prior-Knowledge Questions

1. What does biodiversity mean?
2. How many species of plants are there in the world? In the United States? In the Amazon rainforest or any of its countries?
3. Answer the above question, but using a different group of organisms (birds, insects, mammals, etc.).
4. Which South American country has the highest diversity of bird species?
5. How many tree species are found in an acre of typical U.S. forest? How many have been found in an acre of Amazon rainforest?
6. What portion or percent of all known animal and plant species on Earth are found in the Amazon rainforest?
7. Why are there so many more species of plants and animals found in the rainforest?
8. Explain what endemism or an endemic species is?
9. Define an ecological niche.
10. Define a food web.

Answers to Prior-Knowledge Questions

1. Biodiversity refers to the variety of living organisms found within a given area or habitat.
2. There are approximately 300,000 plant species in the world, 20,000 in the United States, and 80,000 in the Amazon rainforest.
3. Some examples are: butterflies (1,450 species in Peru/730 species in North America), birds (1,300 species in Ecuador/850 in North America), fish (2,000 species in the Amazon River Basin/250 in the Mississippi River Basin).
4. Colombia.
5. Approximately 5-10 species in a U.S. forest compared to as many as 300 found in an acre of Amazonian forest.
6. Approximately one-third of all known plant and animal species are found in the Amazon rainforest.
7. Several hypotheses exist. Mild seasonality and constant availability of resources. Higher degree of specialization. More species have evolved with less extinction due to the climate. The rainforest is a more complex three-dimensional environment offering more physical places for creatures to live.
8. Endemic describes the situation when a species is found in a particular geographical location and nowhere else. For example, the golden toad is endemic to the Monteverde Cloud Forest.
9. An ecological niche is the role an organism plays in its environment.
10. A food web refers to the feeding relationships within an ecosystem.

Objectives

1. Students will be able to define the term biodiversity.
2. Students will be able to demonstrate their knowledge of tropical forest richness and diversity by citing a specific example of an animal or plant group that is compared in both a tropical and temperate forest.
3. Students will be able to discuss at least one theory of why tropical forests contain much higher diversity.
4. Students will be able to define and discuss the concept of endemism.
5. Students will be able to define and discuss the concept of an ecological niche.
6. Students will be able to define a food web and give an example of one using Amazonian species.

Assessment

1. Give examples of organisms that are more diverse in a tropical rainforest than they are in a temperate U.S. forest. How many more species of each are there in the rainforest? (Twice as many? Five times as many?)
2. Define biodiversity.
3. Explain why biodiversity is higher in a tropical rainforest.
4. Explain what is meant by endemism, giving an example of three endemic species found in the Amazon rainforest.
5. Define what is meant by an ecological niche. Give several examples of an organism and its niche, including both biotic and abiotic interactions.
6. Using Amazonian species, give an example of a food web that could be found in the rainforest. Include mention of trophic levels.
7. Explain why you think it is important (or unimportant) for animals like jaguars or harpy eagles to exist even if you will never see one in your lifetime.

Activities

1. Make a bar graph that compares the number of species of certain organisms in U.S. or North American forests with those found in the Amazon rainforest, or in any South American country. You could compare birds, reptiles, amphibians, fish, mammals, insects (or a particular groups of insects), trees, plants, etc.
2. Go to a wooded natural area approved by your teacher. Measure out a meter square on the forest floor and go through it with gloves and garden tools to see what creatures are living in it. Do this activity as a group and have one person record whatever you come upon. (Note: Be careful of snakes, scorpions, spiders, and other things that bite and sting!) Repeat this several times. Which organisms were most plentiful? If you performed this same activity in a tropical forest, what would you expect to find?
3. In the same wooded area, record the species or type of tree (maple, birch, oak, etc.) for each tree that is greater than 10cm in diameter at your eye level. Do this for all trees within a one-acre area. (Your teacher will help you mark it out.) How many different kinds of trees were found? How many (approximately) would you expect to find in an equal-sized area of tropical rainforest?

4. Read *Bats, Bugs, and Biodiversity*. Give a report or presentation on it. What other things could the children in the book have done to learn about the rainforest?

5. Log on to the Internet. See what you can find out about rainforests and biodiversity. (Hint: Look up the names of some of the larger conservation organizations.) Make a list of the Internet addresses that you found useful. Include at least ten.

6. See if it is possible to connect through the Internet to any scientists who are actually doing studies in the rainforest now. Document how you found out about such scientists and what you did to try to contact them. (Hint: You might start by contacting the JASON Foundation (see page 96).

7. Read the book *The Most Beautiful Roof In The World*. Write a report or give a presentation to the class.

8. Army ants are often a visible component of many Amazonian rainforest communities. If a disease wiped out all the army ants in the Amazon Basin, how would it affect other organisms? What if all the katydids were eliminated instead of army ants?

9. There are over 500 species of passion vine plants. How would the Amazon's wildlife be affected if all of these species were eliminated?

10. Compare and contrast several food webs found in the rainforests of South America with food webs found in the temperate forests of North America. Make pyramid charts of the trophic levels with species from each location side by side.

11. Find 'Dr. Canopy' and ask him/her a question. Print out your answer. (Hint: Start on the Internet at: www.evergreen.edu.ican)

Materials

Reference books, paper, graph paper, pen/pencils, Internet access, meter stick, large trays, garden hand tools, flagging tape, Sharpie marking pen, large forceps, and gloves.

Resources

Books
Bats, Bugs, and Biodiversity   (Juvenile)
Susan E. Goodman and Michael J. Doolittle
Antheneum Books for Young Readers
Simon and Schuster   New York, N.Y.
1995   ISBN 0-689-31943-6

The Most Beautiful Roof In The World   (Juvenile)
Kathryn Lasky
Harcourt Brace and Co.   San Diego, CA
1997   ISBN 0-15-200897-7

Living Treasure - Saving Earth's Threatened Biodiversity
Laurence Pringle   (Juvenile)
Morrow Junior Books   New York, N.Y.
1991   ISBN 0-688-07709-9

Wildlife Of The Rainforest   (Juvenile)
Andrew W. Mitchell
Oxford Scientific Films
Colour Library Books, Ltd.   Great Britain
1989   ISBN 0-86283-696-4

Jaguar In The Rain Forest   (Juvenile)
Joanne Ryder
William Morrow & Co.   New York, N.Y.
1996   ISBN 0-688-12990-0

Rainforest Wildlife   (Juvenile)
Antonia Cunningham
Usborne Publishing Ltd.   London, U.K.
1993   ISBN 0-7460-0940-2

Rain Forest   (Juvenile)
Barbara Taylor
Dorling Kindersley, Inc.   New York, N.Y.
1992   ISBN 1-879431-91-2

Life In The Rainforests   (Juvenile)
Lucy Baker
World Book, Inc.   Chicago, IL
1997   ISBN 0-7166-5205-6

Jaguar   (Juvenile)
Roland Smith
Disney Book Publishing   New York, N.Y.
1997   ISBN 0-7868-1312-1

Life In The Treetops
Margaret D. Lowman
Yale Univ. Press　　　　　New Haven, CT
1999　　　　ISBN　0-300-07818-8

Biodiversity
Edward O. Wilson (Editor)
National Academy Press　　Washington, D.C.
1988　　　　ISBN　0-309-03739-5

Biodiversity II
Edward O. Wilson
National Academy Press　　Washington, D.C.
1988　　　　ISBN　0-309-05227-0

Life Above The Jungle Floor
Donald Perry
Simon and Schuster　　　New York, N.Y.
1986　　　　ISBN　0-671-64426-2

The Emerald Realm
Special Publications Division
National Geographic Society　Washington, D.C.
1991　　　　ISBN　0-87044-790-4

The Enchanted Canopy
Andrew W. Mitchell
Macmillan Publishing Co.　　New York, N.Y.
1986　　　　ISBN　0-02-585420-8

Protecting Endangered Species
F. Brooks
Usborne Publishing Ltd.　　London, England
1990　　　　ISBN　0-88110-500-7

Man, Fishes, And The Amazon
Nigel J. Smith
Columbia Univ. Press　　New York, N.Y.
1981　　　　ISBN　0-231-05156-5

High Frontier
Mark W. Moffett
Harvard University Press   Cambridge, MA
1994   ISBN 0-674-39038-5

Forest Canopies
Margaret D. Lowman and Nalini M. Nadkarni
Academic Press   San Diego, CA
1996   ISBN 0-12-457651-6

Birds Of Venezuela
Meyer de Schauensee, William H. Phelps, Jr. and Guy Tudor
Princeton University Press   Princeton, N.J.
1978   ISBN 0-691-08205-7

Neotropical Rainforest Mammals
Louise H. Emmons
U. of Chicago Press   Chicago, IL
1990   ISBN 0-226-20718-8

Butterflies Of South America
Bernard D'Abrera
Hill House
1984   ISBN 0-9593639-2-0

The Venemous Reptiles of Latin America
Jonathan A. Campbell and William W. Lamar
Cornell University Press   Ithaca, N.Y.
1989   ISBN 0-8014-2059-8

Guide To The Frogs Of The Iquitos Region, Amazonian Peru
Lily O. Rodriguez and William E. Duellman
University of Kansas   Lawrence, KS
1994   ISBN 0-89338-047-4

Latin American Insects And Entomology
Charles L. Hogue
U. of California Press   Berkeley, CA
1993   ISBN 0-520-07849-7

Magazine Articles
Biodiversity
National Geographic Magazine
February 1999   Entire Issue

Fire Spares Freed Golden Lion Tamarins
National Geographic Magazine
October 1990   Geographica

An Ecological Probe Of Brazil's Jaguars
National Geographic Magazine
February 1990   Geographica

Patagonia Puma: The Lord Of Land's End
National Geographic Magazine
January 1991   Pages: 102-113

Rain Forest Canopy: The High Frontier
National Geographic Magazine
December 1991   Pages: 78-107

Unusual Mammals Are Bred As Rain Forest Resource
National Geographic Magazine
July 1990   Earth Almanac

A Raft Atop The Rain Forest
National Geographic Magazine
October 1990   Pages: 129-138

From The Amazon: Face Of A New Species
National Geographic Magazine
March 1993   Earth Almanac

How Many Species Exist?
National Wildlife
Dec./Jan. 1999   Pages: 32-33

Videos (see page 16)

Learning Station Four

Economic Botany
Plants for People

Rationale

Species of plants from the rainforest, or that are cultivated in South America, are consumed or used by millions of North Americans daily. This learning station will give students an appreciation for the importance of plants and plant products that form a part of our daily life. In particular, the role that plants play as food crops, spices and condiments, sources of medicine, and for construction or industrial purposes will be discussed. A greater understanding and appreciation of cultural differences will also hopefully result from learning about how various plants are used in different societies and cultures. For example, cocaine is a word that carries a high negative conotation due to its abuse in developed nations. However, the coca plant has been used in a beneficial manner by Andean Indians for thousands of years to help alleviate hunger, increase stamina, and tolerate a high altitude existence.

Prior-Knowledge Questions

1. What is an ethnobotanist? Can you name one?
2. Can you name any nuts, spices, fruits, and/or foods in the super-market that come from South America?
3. What is the difference between cacao, cocaine, coca, and coconuts?
4. Who do you think knows the most about rainforest plants?
5. Can you name any medicines that come from South America, or from a rainforest anywhere in the world?
6. What is a *shaman* or *curandero* or *brujo*?
7. What crop feeds more people in the world than any other?
8. What is curare? Where does it come from?
9. Where does tapioca come from?
10. Who was Richard Evans Schultes?

Answers to Prior-Knowledge Questions

1. An ethnbotanist studies plants that are important to people by living with the people who use them.
2. Brazil nuts, cashews, vanilla, manioc, tomatoes, potatoes.
3. Cacao is the name of the tree that gives us chocolate. Cocaine is the chemical derived from the leaves of the coca plant, or the drug that is made from that chemical. Coconuts are edible palm fruits.
4. The people that use these plants every day, such as the tribes that live in tropical forests and their medicine men.
5. Rosy periwinkle from Madagascar yields a medicine that treats a cancer. Cinchona bark was used to make quinine to treat malaria. The cat's claw vine (*uña de gato*) is used to treat many illnesses. Curare is used as a muscle relaxant and to treat multiple sclerosis and Parkinson's disease.
6. These are all Spanish words that refer to a medicine man or healer.
7. Rice.
8. Curare is a drug that comes from a jungle vine. It causes muscles to stop working.
9. Tapioca comes from the root of the manioc or cassava plant.
10. Richard Evans Schultes was a Harvard professor and one of the most recognized ethnobotanists that ever lived. He spent 1941-1953 in the tropical forests of Colombia and the Amazon Basin exploring for medicinal and useful plants.

Objectives

1. Students will be able to name at least one edible plant native to South America from the following groups: fruits, vegetables, roots or tubers, nuts, and spices or flavorings.
2. Students will learn the historical background of either chocolate, vanilla, or coffee.
3. Students will be able to name the crop that feeds the most people in the world, and the crops most commonly grown in South America.
4. Students will be able to name at least three plants that originate in the rainforest and have medicinal uses or applications.
5. Students will be able to define and distinguish between coca, cocoa, and cocaine.
6. Students will be able to define ehtnobotanist and give two examples.
7. Students will be able to discuss rosy periwinkle and its significance.

8. Students will be able to define and discuss kapok and rubber.
9. Students will be able to discuss the importance and value of rain-forests based on specific examples of products that are of medical, agricultural, or industrial importance.
10. Students will consider cultural differences and how they affect our acceptance of food items and various medicines.

Assessment

1. Name one edible plant from each of the following groups that is native to South America: fruits, vegetables, roots or tubers, nuts, and spices or flavorings.
2. Pick one of the following and write a brief paper on its history and use: coffee, chocolate, or vanilla.
3. Take one of the above items and write an essay on what life would be like if it didn't exist.
4. What crop feeds more people in the world than any other?
5. What three crops are most commonly consumed in South America?
6. Name three rainforest plants that have medicinal uses and explain what those uses are.
7. Distinguish between coca, cocoa, and cocaine.
8. What is an ethnobotanist? Name two of them.
9. What is the rosy periwinkle? Where is it found? What is its signifi-cance to human health?
10. What is kapok? What is/was it used for?
11. Where does natural rubber come from? How is it harvested?
12. With synthetic rubber available today, is there any need for natural rubber? If so, for what?
13. Compare and contrast the importance of cassava and coffee to the countries and people of South America.
14. Explain the effect that the demand for the illegal drug cocaine by people in the U.S. has had on the rainforest and its peoples in South America.
15. Discuss why in this age of world commerce, rapid transportation, and refrigeration many South American commodities like cashew apples, passion fruits, and guarana are almost unknown in the United States.
16. Describe how you think Amazonian Indians first learned about the properties of medicinal plants.

Activities

1. After looking through the materials at this learning station, go to the supermarket and make a list of all the South American food items you can find there. Indicate which ones you've eaten yourself.
2. Select either chocolate, vanilla, or coffee and research its history and use. Describe what you think would happen if production of this commodity were cut in half.
3. Do a brief report or presentation on the cultivation of rice.
4. Go to the supermarket and see if you can find any items with passion fruit or guarana in them. (Hint: You might try looking at the juices or soft drinks.)
5. Go to the supermarket and compare the prices of peanuts, cashews, and Brazil nuts. Which is the most expensive? Why do you think it costs more?
6. Do a brief report or presentation on the plant called 'cat's claw' or *uña de gato*. (Hint: You might start at a health food store.)
7. Do a brief report or presentation on the history and use of quinine.
8. Define, compare and contrast cocoa, coca, and cocaine.
9. Read *The Shaman's Apprentice* and report on it.
10. Watch the movie *Medicine Man*. Give your reaction to the movie. What parts, if any, did you have trouble believing?
11. Write a brief report on either Richard Spruce, Richard Evans Schultes, Wade Davis, Nicole Maxwell, Mark Plotkin, or Jim Duke.
12. Research the importance and significance of the rosy periwinkle.
13. Do a report or presentation on the history and use of either kapok or rubber.
14. Go to a pharmacy and list at least five over-the-counter medicines that contain materials from rainforest plants. How can you determine whether a medicine contains such materials or not?
15. Compare and contrast the use of medicinal plants by South American Indians with their use by North American Indians.
16. Compare and contrast a medicinal plant found and used only in the Amazon with a medicinal plant found and used only in North America.
17. You have been given the assignment of going to the Amazon for a year and prospecting for plants that may have medicinal properties. Explain briefly how you would go about this. Include an explanantion of how you would confirm whether or not a plant really had medicinal potential or not.

Materials

Books, posters, videos, magazine articles, newspaper clippings, fresh tropical food items from the supermarket, juice or food containers with tropical plants as part of the ingredients, and tropical spices or condiments.

Resources

Books

The Shaman's Apprentice   (Juvenile)
Lynne Cherry and Mark J. Plotkin
Harcourt Brace & Co.   San Diego, CA
1998   ISBN 0-15-201281-8

Plants For People
Anna Lewington
Oxford University Press   New York, N.Y.
1990   ISBN 0-19-520840-4

Economic Botany - Plants In Our World
Beryl B. Simpson and Molly C. Ogorzaly
McGraw-Hill   New York, N.Y.
1995   ISBN 0-07-057569-X

Tropical Forests And Their Crops
Nigel J.H. Smith, J.T. Williams, Donald L. Plucknett, Jennifer P. Talbot
Cornell University Press   Ithaca, N.Y.
1992   ISBN 0-8014-8058-2

Chilies To Chocolate
Nelson Foster and Linda S. Cordell (Editors)
U. of Arizona Press   Tucson, AZ
1992   ISBN 0-8165-1324-4

Rainforest Remedies
Rosita Arvigo and Michael Balick
Lotus Press   Twin Lakes, WI
1993   ISBN 0-914955-13-6

Books (cont.)

The Healing Forest
Richard E. Schultes and Robert F. Raffauf
Dioscorides Press   Portland, OR
1990   ISBN 0-931146-14-3

A Field Guide To Medicinal And Useful Plants Of The Upper Amazon
James L. Castner, Stephen L. Timme, and James A. Duke
Feline Press   Gainesville, FL
1998   ISBN 0-9625150-7-8

Amazonian Ethnobotanical Dictionary
James A. Duke and Rodolfo Vasquez
CRC Press   Boca Raton, FL
1994   ISBN 0-8493-3664-3

How Indians Use Wild Plants For Food, Medicine & Crafts
Frances Densmore
Dover Publications   New York, N.Y.
1974   ISBN 0-486-23019-8

Plants, People, And Culture
Michael J. Balick and Paul A. Cox
Scientific American Library   New York, N.Y.
1996   ISBN 0-7167-6027-4

Plants, Man And Life
Edgar Anderson
Missouri Botanical Garden   St. Louis, MO
1997   ISBN 0-915279-44-4

Trees Of Life
Kenton Miller and Laura Tangley
Beacon Press   Boston, MA
1991   ISBN 0-8070-8505-7

The Green Pharmacy
James A. Duke
St. Martin's Paperbacks   New York, N.Y.
1998   ISBN 0-312-96648-2

Healing Herbs
Michael Castleman
Bantam Books   New York, N.Y.
1995   ISBN 0-553-56988-0

Earthly Goods
Christopher Joyce
Little, Brown and Co.   Boston, MA
1994   ISBN 0-316-47408-8

Medicinal Resources Of The Tropical Forest
Michael J. Balick, Elaine Elisabetsky and Sarah A. Laird (Editors)
Columbia University Press   New York, N.Y.
1996   ISBN 0-231-10171-6

Wizard Of The Upper Amazon
F. Bruce Lamb
North Atlantic Books   Berkeley, CA
1974   ISBN 0-938190-80-6

Witch-Doctor's Apprentice
Nicole Maxwell
Citadell Press   New York, N.Y.
1990   ISBN 0-8065-1174-5

Tales Of A Shaman's Apprentice
Mark J. Plotkin
Penguin Books   New York, N.Y.
1993   ISBN 0-14-012991-X

One River
Wade Davis
Simon and Schuster   New York, N.Y.
1996   ISBN 0-684-83496-0

Books (cont.)
Vine Of The Soul
Richard E. Schultes and Robert F. Raffauf
Synergetic Press   Synerg, AZ
1992   ISBN 0-907791-24-7

National Geographic Society Publications
An Ancient Indian Herb Turns Deadly: Coca
National Geographic Magazine
January 1989   Pages: 3-47

The Plant Hunters: A Portrait Of The Missouri Botanical Garden
National Geographic Magazine
August 1990   Pages: 124-140

Nuts To Ivory, Carved Seeds Help Save Forest
National Geographic Magazine
February 1991   Earth Almanac

Animals Heal Themselves With Nature's Pharmacy
National Geographic Magazine
January 1993   Earth Almanac

My, Oh, Maya, How They Loved Chocolate
National Geographic Magazine
March 1991   Geographica

Spain In The Americas: The Grand Exchange
National Geographic Society Map
February 1992

Other Publications
A Tropical Feast Flashcard Set
Missouri Botanical Garden Education Division
St. Louis, MO
Phone: (314)-577-5100

The Medicinal Plants Information Center at:
www.medicinalplantinfo.com

Learning Station Five

Camouflage and Mimicry
Now you see it, now you don't!

Rationale

The theme of camouflage and mimicry is an excellent way to expose students to biological and ecological concepts including evolution, natural selection, and predator/prey relationships. It can also be used to introduce the study of animal behavior while serving to reinforce the theme of diversity. The tactics and strategies used by exotic tropical insects and organisms are the same as those used by many of the more common insects of the United States. They are therefore easily illustrated with local examples and can be made directly relevant to almost all curricula in the life sciences. This learning station will also serve to develop the students' powers of observation, resulting in them looking at the natural world around them in a more probing and analytical manner.

Prior-Knowledge Questions

1. What kind of colors do bumble bees and other stinging insects have?
2. Name any two animals that protect themselves with camouflage.
3. Can you give an example of one animal that mimics or imitates another animal?
4. When are most camouflaged insects active?
5. Do you know who Fritz Müller or Henry Walter Bates were?
6. How does a praying mantis move? Why?
7. Can you name any insects in the United States that look like a leaf? Or a twig? Or a bird dropping? Or a snake? Or a thorn?
8. Can you name any insect in the United States that has bright colors but doesn't sting? How do you think it protects itself?
9. Can you name any insects in the United States that have eyespots on their wings or bodies?
10. Can you name any animals that 'play dead'?

Answers to Prior-Knowledge Questions

1. Colors that contrast with one another, that make them easy to see and easy to recognize.
2. Grasshoppers, caterpillars, frogs, deer, stink bugs, etc.
3. Many flies imitate bees or wasps. Some moths imitate wasps.
4. Usually at night.
5. Both were naturalists who worked in the Amazon Basin during the 1800's. Both made significant contributions to the study of animal mimicry.
6. With a slow, swaying motion like a twig being gently moved around by a breeze. Their movements are not sudden, but 'natural'.
7. Some butterflies when their wings are closed look like a leaf. Some caterpillars and walkingsticks look like twigs. Some moths and caterpillars are colored like bird droppings. Some caterpillars resemble snakes. One species of treehopper has the appearance of a thorn.
8. The monarch butterfly and its caterpillar, which feeds on milkweed. The oleander moth and its caterpillar, which feeds on oleander. These creatures protect themselves with chemicals they ingest from their food plants.
9. The io moth and the spicebush swallowtail caterpillar are two.
10. Walkingsticks will play dead, as will opossums and hog-nose snakes.

Objectives

1. Students will be able to name and describe the major categories of protective coloration.
2. Students will be able to name one or more insects/animals from their own geographical region (or the United States) that represent the above categories.
3. Students will be able to explain how the behavior of organisms with adaptive coloration has evolved to complement the particular type of protective coloring they exhibit.
4. Students will be able to define primary and secondary defense mechanisms and provide examples of each.
5. Students will be able to define Batesian and Müllerian mimicry, provide examples, and explain the ecological concepts upon which the theories are based.

Assessment

1. Name and explain three of the types of camouflage and mimicry or protective coloration.
2. Give at least one example for each of the above categories of a local insect or animal that uses that kind of protection.
3. Explain how specific behaviors of the animals listed above in question # 2 help them to avoid predators.
4. You are taking a survival course and as the final exam you have been transported and dropped in a wooded area that is similar to a forest on Earth. The main predator in the forest is the 'arnator'. It is a large, fast-moving, sharp-fanged creature that is active during the day, but doesn't move around much at night. To pass the test, you only have to survive for the one week before you are picked up and taken back to Earth. How will you avoid being eaten by the arnator? If the test lasted a full year, what do you think would happen to some of the other students taking this final exam? (Based on Robert Heinlein's story *Tunnel In The Sky.*)
5. Distinguish between a primary and secondary defense mechanism, giving three examples of each.
6. The first explorers on Mars find a fierce animal that is ten feet tall, has bright orange and blue markings, and squirts a deadly acid on anything that comes near it. Describe the characteristics of both the Batesian and Müllerian mimics of this creature.

Activities

1. Review the information and materials provided and write down at least five different types of strategies used in protective coloration.
2. Draw five different creatures that use each of these strategies. (Do not worry about how realistic your picture looks, but include some details.)
3. If you were to be an insect for 24 hours, which type of protective coloration would you prefer? Write a short story about one day and one night in your life, telling what you did, how you acted, and why. Include a confrontation with a predator.
4. Give a brief biographical report/presentation/play on the life of either Henry Walter Bates or Fritz Müller.

5. In the area of your school grounds (or at a park or approved natural area), try to locate as many insects/animals with protective coloration as possible. Make a list of what you see. Record the animal's color, shape, appearance, and the place where you found it (on a leaf, the ground, a twig, etc.). You may work in groups.

6. Select an insect that survives by some type of camouflage. How would you test to make sure this was actually what was happening? Design an experiment to do so.

7. Select an insect that survives by tasting bad. How would you test that this is really what is occurring? Design an experiment to do so.

8. Draw a series of three new animals that mimic household or manufactured objects. Be sure you can make out all the basic anatomical parts of the animal (legs, eyes, ears, antennae, etc.).

9. Present a short skit where one person plays a protectively-colored insect and another person plays some type of predator. Demonstrate the insect's behavior before the predator sees it and after the predator attacks it.

10. Name ten creatures in your backyard that might have protective coloration, and tell what kind they would have.

11. Name several predators that camouflage would be no protection against. Why wouldn't it work against these predators?

12. Make up a game where there is one predator and five or six prey, each with its own different protective strategy. Explain and demonstrate the game.

13. Take five leaves that have different shapes from the school yard or park. Trace their outline on a piece of paper. Make a leaf-mimicking insect out of each, drawing in the legs, eyes, antennae, wings, etc. Color each creature differently, but in a way that you think would effectively camouflage it. (They do not have to match the original leaf.)

14. Pick two of the camouflaged insects available in photographs and make replicas of them as closely as you can using the natural objects they imitate. For example, if one of the insects looks like a pointed green leaf with brown twig-like legs, find a pointed green leaf (or cut one) and attach small twigs as legs.

Materials

Books, magazine articles, videos, paper, pens/pencils (colored), slide sets (35mm transparencies), and an insect collection.

Resources
Books
Look Again!   (Juvenile)
Dial Book for Young Readers
New York, N.Y.
1992   ISBN 0-8037-0958-7

Usborne Mysteries And Marvels Of Insect Life   (Juvenile)
Jennifer Owen
Usborne Publishing   London, U.K.
1989   ISBN 0-8620-843-5

Camouflage And Mimicry
Denis Owen
U. of Chicago Press   Chicago, IL
1980   ISBN 0-226-64188-0

Camouflage And Color - Strategies For Survival
Liz Bomford
Dorset Press   New York, N.Y.
1992   ISBN 0-88029-923-1

Magazine Articles
Please Don't Eat The Katydids
James L. Castner
International Wildlife Magazine
May/June 1998

Freeloading Caterpillars Masquerade As Ants
National Geographic Magazine
December 1991   Earth Almanac

How To Fool A Piranha: Two Heads Are Better Than One
National Geographic Magazine
November 1992   Geographica

Its A Twig, A Catkin . . . No! Its A Caterpillar
National Geographic Magazine
October 1989   Geographica

Rainforest Destruction
Where is it going?

Rationale
The Amazon Basin contains the single largest extant area of tropical rainforest in the world, yet it continues to disappear at an alarming rate. Like the world's oceans, it too is finite and fragile, susceptible to the influences of humans. There are numerous factors that contribute to the destruction of tropical forests, some of which are directly related to consumer behavior in developed countries like the United States and Japan. It is important for students to understand that there is no easy answer on how to halt the destruction of tropical forests. Exposure to this learning station will induce them to think about the factors that contribute to rainforest destruction and how they relate to one another. Understanding such interaction is the basic knowledge necessary for any attempt to resolve the situation.

Prior-Knowledge Questions
1. Why are the rainforests all over the world being destroyed?
2. How can we measure such destruction?
3. What happens when a major river in a forest is dammed?
4. What is an endangered species?
5. What is extinction? What causes extinction? Have any animals in the United States become extinct during the past 200 years? If yes, what were they?
6. What is global warming? What causes it?
7. Does what you do and what you buy here in the United States have any effect on rainforests? How?
8. If you owned land with beautiful trees on it, but someone offered you a lot of money to cut it and plant tobacco, what would you do?
9. In a remote tropical forest a tree is discovered whose sap contains chemical properties that fight the AIDS virus. What do you think should be done with the forest where that tree is found? Who do you think should benefit (financially) from the development of any medicines or products from that tree?

10. You have a bristlecone pine tree that is 4,000 years old growing on your property. A collector wants it and is willing to pay you $100,000 for it. Would you sell it? Why or why not?
11. You have a very rare bird that is nesting in a tree in your backyard. A man who collects bird skins wants to kill it and stuff it. He will pay you $100,000 for the right to do so. Will you let him?
12. Has 'El Niño' had any effect on the Amazon rainforest?

Answers To Prior-Knowledge Questions
1. They are being cut for cattle grazing, lumber, and as part of slash and burn agriculture.
2. High altitude photography clearly shows deforestation and fires that are burning in the Amazon.
3. The area behind the dam is flooded, destroying the forest.
4. An endangered species has so few individuals left that they may not be able to continue breeding. Extinction is when the last individual of a species dies and none are left.
5. Extinction when applied to animals means that there are none left or that they no longer exist. Some causes of extinction are habitat loss, hunting, and natural catastrophes. The passenger pigeon and dusky seaside sparrow are two U.S. species that have become recently extinct.
6. Global warming is an increase in the Earth's average temperature due to a build-up of certain gases trapped in the atmosphere.
7. Yes. For example, some fast food restaurants have routinely bought beef from cattle raised where rainforests had been cleared to make pastures. The beef was cheaper, but our consumer habits had a direct negative effect on the amount of deforestation in certain areas.
10. Yes. El Niño has caused droughts resulting in much more extensive fires in the rainforest.

Objectives
1. Students will be able to state and discuss the major causes of rainforest destruction (ex. overpopulation, cattle grazing, lumbering).
2. Students will be able to give examples of how the actions and policies of people in developed/industrial countries affect the actions and policies of people in developing countries (such as the ones where most rainforests exist).

3. Students will be able to define endangered species.
4. Students will be able to define extinction and discuss its causes.
5. Students will be able to define extractive reserve.
6. Students will be able to discuss the concept of sustainability.

Assessment

1. Give five examples of activities that result in the destruction of tropical forests.
2. Give two examples of things we do in the United States that can result in having a negative effect on tropical forests.
3. Define the term endangered species. List at least five species of organisms from the tropics that fit in this category.
4. Define the term extinction. List three causes of extinction and organisms that have become extinct due to each.
5. Define the term extractive reserve and give an example.
6. Explain in your own words the concept of sustainability. What forest uses are considered sustainable? Why are sustainable operations considered a better way to make use of rainforests?
7. Calculate the life expectancy of the Amazon rainforest based on the current levels of destruction.
8. Compare and contrast conservation and lumbering policies of the United States regarding its old growth forests in the Northwest with the South American country of your choice.
9. Evaluate the country of Brazil with regards to its rainforest policies.
10. Explain the difference between the regeneration and regrowth of a rainforest after small-scale farming by Indians as compared to large-scale cutting for timber purposes.
11. Discuss the reasons that gold mining can be detrimental to rainforest areas, citing actual examples from articles you've read.

Activities

1. Read some of the articles and information provided. List at least five major causes of rainforest destruction. Which of these do you think would be the easiest to stop or change? Why? Report on how you would accomplish this.
2. Find out if there are any organizations dedicated to saving the rainforest. Make a list of them and how to contact them. How do they suggest stopping rainforest destruction?

3. Get together with some of your classmates (either one on one, or in small groups) and have a debate about the use and exploitation of the rainforest. (Suggestions: Divide up into sides that represent conservationists vs. timber company, or rubber tapper vs. cattle rancher.)

4. Do a report/presentation on the tropical fish industry and/or tropical bird industry and its effects. If there is a store that sells such animals in your town, call them and ask them the source of their animals.

5. Do a report/presentation on how the cultivation of coca has affected the rainforest.

6. Define 'ecotourism' and tell if you think it is a good thing or a bad thing. Defend your answer.

7. Read an article on endangered species. List at least ten such species. What species are endangered in the United States? Have any become extinct in the last hundred years? Should we care? Why? Report/present your findings and opinion.

8. Read about the harvesting of rubber and Brazil nuts. Explain how these commodities relate to the concept of an extractive reserve.

Materials

Rainforest conservation brochures, rainforest conservation posters, reference books, magazine articles, and newspaper clippings.

Resources
Books

South American Monkeys - Endangered! Series   (Juvenile)
A. Harman
Marshall Cavendish   Tarrytown, N.Y.
1996   ISBN 0-7614-0218-7

Parrots - Endangered! Series   (Juvenile)
C. Horton
Marshall Cavendish   Tarrytown, N.Y.
1996   ISBN 0-7614-0222-5

Grolier World Encyclopedia Of Endangered Species
South America I and II
Grolier Educational Corp.   Bethel, CT
1993   ISBN 0-7172-7192-7

Books (cont.)
Lessons Of The Rainforest
Suzanne Head and Robert Heinzman (Editors)
Sierra Club Books   San Francisco, CA
1990   ISBN 0-87156-682-6

Tropical Rainforests
James D. Nations
Franklin Watts   New York, N.Y.
1988   ISBN 0-531-10604-7

Sustainable Harvest And Marketing Of Rain Forest Products
Mark Plotkin and Lisa Famolare (Editors)
Island Press   Washington, D.C.
1992   ISBN 1-55963-168-6

Magazine Articles
The Assault Continues
International Wildlife
Nov./Dec. 1998   Pages: 44-51

New Sensors Eye The Rainforest
National Geographic Magazine
September 1993   Pages: 118-130

Amazon's Gold Rush Spills Deadly Quicksilver
National Geographic Magazine
June 1992   Earth Almanac

Forest's Living History Imperiled By Logging
National Geographic Magazine
September 1991   Geographica

Endangered Species Issue   (Juvenile)
Kids Discover
June/July 1995
Phone: (212)-242-5133

People and Their Languages
Who's who?

Rationale
Many students are unfamiliar with the variety of languages that are spoken in South America. Indigenous tribes and their dialects are seldom included or considered an integral part of the population of the continent. Other students may be unaware that familiar languages (including English) other than Spanish are spoken in several countries. At least five major world languages are spoken in South America. This learning station will inform students about the many Indian tribes that exist on the continent. It shall also result in their recognizing that a number of world languages are spoken there. This information can tie in nicely with the historical exploration and colonization of the South American continent.

Prior-Knowledge Questions
1. How many languages are spoken in South America?
2. Did you include Indian dialects in your answer above?
3. Do you consider people in the United States who speak English with a heavy foreign accent to be less intelligent than those that don't?
4. Name five Indian tribes from North America. Name five from South America.
5. If you were sick and needed help in a foreign country and couldn't speak the language, what would you do?
6. What does the word 'Hispanic' mean?
7. Many of the South American Indians that live in the rainforest cannot read. Does that make them less intelligent than we?
8. Some Amazonian Indians wear feathers in their noses and big wooden plugs in their ear lobes. Are they less intelligent than we?
9. Why did early explorers go to South America?
10. If a pharmaceutical company with the help of an Indian medicine man discovers a forest plant that eventually yields a new drug, do you think the Indian will get any of the money from the sales?

Answers To Prior-Knowledge Questions

1. There are five major world languages spoken as the national languages of the countries of South America. Additionally, there are dozens of Indian dialects spoken.
4. Cheyenne, Sioux, Crow, Hopi, and Navajo (and many others) in North America. Yanomami, Yagua, Witoto, Jivaro, and Kayapó (and many others) in South America.
6. Hispanic means many things to many people. One definition is a person whose recent ancestors are from Spanish-speaking countries in Central or South America.
9. Early explorers sought gold and a shorter trade route to the Indies.

Objectives

1. Students will be able to identify the major world language spoken in each South American country, as well as the European country that originally colonized it.
2. Students will be able to name a different indigenous Indian group or tribe for each of five countries of South America.
3. Students will be able to define the following vocabulary words: Indian, mestizo, negro, African, mulatto, Spanish, Hispanic, Latin American, American.
4. Students will be able to recognize historical similarities in the treatment of indigenous cultures by more technologically-advanced cultures.
5. Students will recognize that geographical differences in linguistics occur within Spanish-speaking cultures just as they do among English-speaking individuals who live in the United States.
6. Students will recognize that Spanish-speaking individuals form a large part of the population in the United States even if they don't live near a large Hispanic population center.

Assessment

1. Fill in on the outline map of South America provided, the major world language that is spoken in each country.
2. On the same map, add the name of the country that originally colonized it.
3. Select any five countries and name at least one Indian tribe or indigenous group of people for each. (Make sure you list five different tribes!)

4. The mixture of Spanish colonists with indigenous Indians and black slaves and settlers has resulted in various combinations of ethnic groups. What are some of the words that describe these mixtures? Define which groups and combinations they indicate.
5. Define the words Hispanic, Spanish, Latin American, African, and American.
6. Compare and contrast slavery of Africans in the U.S. with that of Amerindians in South America during the rubber trade.
7. Calculate what percent of the U.S. population is Hispanic.
8. Compare and contrast the differences in English spoken in the North, South, and Midwest with Spanish spoken in Latin America, Spain, and the Caribbean.

Activities

1. Read a brief history or synopsis of each South American country in one of the references that is provided (atlas, encyclopedia, etc.). Pay attention to what country or world power originally colonized it and how that is reflected in the language and customs that exist there today.
2. Read a National Geographic article on any South American country. Do a brief report/presentation on what you have learned.
3. Log on to the Internet and see what information you can find for at least three South American countries. Submit a brief report that includes web site addresses (URLs).
4. Look at the National Geographic map of South American Indian tribes and their distribution. Try to pronounce their names. Do a brief report on any one tribe.
5. Look up the following list of words in a dictionary and record their definitions: Indian, mestizo, negro, African, mulatto, Spanish, Hispanic, American, Latin American. They describe people that are a mixture of Spanish, Indian, and African descent. What physical characteristics are found in these different people? Look through the reference materials and find an example of each in a photo.
6. Do a brief report on the Summer Institute of Linguistics.

Materials

Atlas, books, National Geographic magazines that cover specific South American countries, and the National Geographic map on the Indian Tribes of South America (March 1982).

Resources
Books
Amazon Diary   (Juvenile)
Hudson Talbott and Mark Greenberg
Putnam & Grosset   New York, N.Y.
1996   ISBN 0-698-11699-2

The Rain Forest Storybook   (Juvenile)
Rosalind Kerven
Cambridge Univ. Press   New York, N.Y.
1994   ISBN 0-521-43533-1

Amazonian Indians   (Juvenile)
Anna Lewington
Marshall Cavendish   Tarrytown, N.Y.
1993   ISBN 0-87226-367-3

Brazil - Cultures Of The World Series   (Juvenile)
C. Richard
Marshall Cavendish   Tarrytown, N.Y.
1991   ISBN 1-85435-3829

Colombia - Cultures Of The World Series   (Juvenile)
J. DuBois
Marshall Cavendish   Tarrytown, N.Y.
1991   ISBN 1-85435-384-5

Venezuela - Cultures Of The World Series (Juvenile)
J. Kohen Winter
Marshall Cavendish   Tarrytown, N.Y.
1991   ISBN 1-85435-386-1

Ecuador - Cultures Of The World Series   (Juvenile)
E. Foley
Marshall Cavendish   Tarrytown, N.Y.
1995   ISBN 0-7614-0173-3

Peru - Cultures Of The World Series   (Juvenile)
K. Falconer
Marshall Cavendish   Tarrytown, N.Y.
1996   ISBN 0-7614-0179-2

Bolivia - Cultures Of The World Series   (Juvenile)
B. Pateman
Marshall Cavendish   Tarrytown, N.Y.
1996   ISBN 0-7614-0178-4

Argentina - Cultures Of The World Series   (Juvenile)
Ethel C. Gofen
Marshall Cavendish   Tarrytown, N.Y.
1991   ISBN 1-85435-381-0

Chile - Cultures Of The World Series   (Juvenile)
J. Kohen Winter
Marshall Cavendish   Tarrytown, N.Y.
1991   ISBN 1-85435-383-7

Amazonia
Betty J. Meggers
Smithsonian Inst. Press   Washington, D.C.
1996   ISBN 1-56098-655-7

People Of The Tropical Rain Forest
Julie S. Denslow and Christine Padoch (Editors)
U. of California Press   Berkeley, CA
1988   ISBN 0520-06351-1

Mekranoti
Gustaaf Verswijver
Prestel-Verlag   Munich, Germany
1996   ISBN 3-7913-1431-9

Amazonian Indians
Anna Roosevelt (Editor)
U. of Arizona Press   Tucson, AZ
1994   ISBN 0-8165-1821-1

Books (cont.)

Xingu - The Indians, Their Myths
Orlando Villas Boas and Claudio Villas Boas
Farrar, Straus and Giroux   New York, N.Y.
1970   ISBN 0-374-29338-4

Mehinaku
Thomas Gregor
U. of Chicago Press   Chicago, IL
1977   ISBN 0-226-30746-8

The Cubeo
Irving Goldman
U. of Illinois Press   Urbana, IL
1979   ISBN 0-252-00770-0

The Enchanted Amazon Rain Forest
Nigel J.H. Smith
U. Press of Florida   Gainesville, FL
1997   ISBN 0-8130-1377-1

Yanomamo - The Fierce People
Napoleon A. Chagnon
Holt, Rinehart and Winston   New York, N.Y.
1983   ISBN 0-03-062328-6

Makuna - Portrait Of An Amazonian People
Kaj Århem
Smithsonian Institution Press Washington, D.C.
1998   ISBN 1-56098-874-6

Handbook Of South American Indians
Julian H. Steward (Editor)
Smithsonian Institution   Washington, D.C.
Bureau of American Ethnology
Bulletin 143
1948

National Geographic Society Publications

Indians / Archaeology Of South America
National Geographic Society Map
March 1982

Gold Rush Destroying A Primitive Culture
National Geographic Magazine
January 1991   Earth Almanac

Cartagena Nights (Colombia)
National Geographic Magazine
April 1989   Pages: 494-509

Emeralds (Colombia)
National Geographic Magazine
July 1990   Pages: 38-69

DNA Profiling: The New Science Of Identity (Argentina)
National Geographic Magazine
May 1992   Pages: 112-124

Plotting A New Course (Paraguay)
National Geographic Magazine
August 1992   Pages: 88-113

A Photographic Gift Of A Venezuelan Trek
National Geographic Magazine
September 1990   Geographica

Venezuela's Islands In Time
National Geographic Magazine
May 1989   Pages: 526-561

Roaring Through Earth's Deepest Canyon (Peru)
National Geographic Magazine
January 1993   Pages: 119-138

60

Learning Station Eight

Art and Artifacts
Baskets, Blowguns, and Shrunken Heads

Rationale
The investigation and examination of art objects and artifacts produced by Amazonian tribes will lead to a greater understanding of these indigenous cultures and their customs. The rainforest provides all the basic materials needed by Amazonian Indians in order to survive in what others might consider a hostile environment. This learning station will provide the opportunity for students to develop an admiration and respect for less technologically advanced cultures that have learned to meet their needs with only the materials available from the environment that surrounds them. With the growth of respect for such cultures, will hopefully come tolerance of individuals whom are different. Excellent parallels can be drawn between South American indigenous cultures and the Indian tribes of North America and/or other geographical areas of the world.

Prior-Knowledge Questions
1. If you wanted to make a ceramic pot, how would you do it?
2. Do you have any natural items in your home that serve a functional use? List several and tell their use.
3. Do you know of any similarities between the Indians of South America and the Indians of North America?
4. What are the basic needs that all human beings have for survival?
5. Going beyond the basic needs, what other things are needed for comfort and enjoyment?
6. What is a calabash? A gourd?
7. Have you ever had to go without electricity for more than a day? What was it like?
8. What do you think it would be like to live in an environment where you had no electricity, no hot water, no appliances, no stores, and you had to make everything you wanted from the materials around you?
9. How would you know if a fruit were safe to eat or not?
10. Do you think there are more Indians living in the Amazon Basin now than a hundred years ago? Why?

Answers To Prior-Knowledge Questions

1. One way is to roll out pieces of clay, coil them, and stack them one on top of the other. (A coil pot.)
3. Weapons, mythology, art and artifacts including ceramics, use of natural items.
4. Food, shelter, protection against the environment.
6. Calabash is a large, thick-skinned fruit of a small tree. A gourd is a thick-skinned fruit of a vine. Both can be used as water dippers.
9. Observe whether or not animals eat it.
10. There are many less Indians today. Their numbers have decreased due to diseases, slavery, and the loss of habitat.

Objectives

1. Students will learn how to make a coil pot, one of the basic ceramic-producing techniques used by people worldwide.
2. Students will be able to define and discuss some of the basic materials used by native groups which originate from the rainforest.
3. Students will be able to discuss how non-industrialized societies have worked out viable, technologically-simple ways to survive in their environment.
4. Students will be able to identify similarities and differences between North American Indians and South American Indians.
5. Students will recognize that cultures widely separated geographically have invented similar tools and implements and have found similar solutions to the problems of everyday living.

Assessment

1. Describe the steps you would follow to make a coil pot. In your description, use and define the following words: coil pot, slip, clay, temper, resin, dye, and glaze.
2. Pick five things or objects that an Amazonian Indian might use in his daily life that originated in the rainforest. Describe what they are, what they are used for, and how they were made.
3. Students taking Spanish give the Spanish words for hammock, blowgun, fiber, and basket.
4. Give an example of how you think Amazonian Indians have proved the old saying that 'necessity is the mother of invention'.
5. Define 'flint knapping' and its significance.
6. Distinguish between a primitive and advanced civilization.

7. Compare and contrast Indian tribes of North America with tribes of South America with respect to shelter, weapons, food, clothing, and transportation. Give reasons for the similarities and differences that you find.
8. Explain why the blowgun only seems to have been invented by forest peoples.
9. Compare and contrast the headhunters of Ecuador (the Jivaro) with the headhunters of Borneo.
10. Explain why almost identical objects have been invented by widely separated peoples.

Activities

1. Use the materials and directions provided to make and decorate a coil pot. If you couldn't buy the materials, how would you make, color, and decorate a clay pot?
2. Walk through the school yard (or a park or approved natural area) and collect natural things/objects that you could use in your daily life. Tell what function they would have or how you would use them.
3. Watch one of the rainforest documentaries available and describe how the inhabitants are able to live without electricity or manufactured items.
4. Amazonian Indians sometimes make jewelry out of colorful seeds, feathers, or insects. Are there any of these materials where you live that you could use to make jewelry? Draw a picture of the object you would make and label the natural materials that you would use. If the items are easily available, go ahead and make the object you have in mind. (Caution: Some brightly-colored seeds are poisonous so be careful not to leave them around small children or pets, and be sure not to eat any of them! Wash your hands when done.)
5. Research and report on the similarities and differences between North American Indians and South American Indians. Consider things such as shelter, clothing, weapons, modes of travel, art and decorations, etc.
6. Describe in a short story or fictional diary how you survived for six months in the Amazon jungle after your plane crashed and left you there alone.

7. You are kidnapped by Amazonian Indians! Describe in a fictional journal what it is like to live with them.
8. Make a functional object from a natural object that is easily available (ex. a water dipper from a gourd).
9. What is *chambira* fiber? Where does it come from? What items are commonly made from it?
10. Describe a single day in the life of an Amazonian Indian, paying special attention to natural products that might be used in a day.
11. What is a *tipiti*? What is it used for? (Hint: It is related to manioc.)
12. Describe a native blowgun, darts, quiver, fletching, and tell where all the materials came from that were used to make them.
13. Which South American Indians shrunk the heads of their enemies? Why? How did they do it? Write a brief report on it.
14. Do a brief report on 'flint knapping'. Mention the use of arrowheads and stone points in determining the times when various tribes lived in North America. Discuss why there are so few stone points from the Amazon Basin and tell what Amazonian Indians used in their place.

Materials

Clay, paper, pen/pencil, reference books, videos and rainforest documentaries, and a VCR.

Resources
Books
Latin American And Caribbean Crafts   (Juvenile)
Judith H. Corwin
Franklin Watts   New York, N.Y.
1992   ISBN 0-531-11014-1

Arts And Crafts Of South America
Lucie Davies and Mo Finey
Chronicle Books   San Francisco, CA
1994   ISBN 0811808122

Arts Of The Amazon
Barbara Braun (Editor)
Thames and Hudson Ltd.   London, U.K.
1995   ISBN 0-500-27824-5

Books (cont.)
Baskets
Meryl Doney
Franklin Watts   Danbury, CT
1997   ISBN 0-531-14445-3

Basketry As Metaphor
Gerardo Reichel-Dolmatoff
Museum of Cultural History
U. of California   Los Angeles, CA
1985   ISBN 0-930741-03-X

Discovering The Folk Art Of Latin America
Marion Oettinger, Jr.
Junior Penguin Group   Bergenfield, N.J.
1992   ISBN 0525934359

Kaiapó
Gustaaf Verwijver (Editor)
Royal Museum for Central Africa (Tervuren)
Snoeck-Ducaju & Zoon   Gent, Belgium
1992

The Gift Of Birds
Ruben E. Reina and Kenneth M. Kensinger (Editors)
University Museum of Archaeology and Anthropology
U. of Pennsylvania   Philadelphia, PA
1991   ISBN 0-924171-12-X

l'art de la plume brésil
MUSEE D' ETHNOGRAPHIE - GENEVE
1985   Geneva, Switzerland

*Stone Age Spear And Arrow Points Of The Midcontinental
And Eastern United States*
Noel D. Justice
Indiana University Press   Bloomington, IN
1987   ISBN 0-253-35406-4

Costumes & Featherwork Of The Lords Of Chimor
The Textile Museum   Washington, D.C.
1984   ISBN 0-81405-023-5

From Myth To Creation
Dorothea S. Whitten and Norman E. Whitten, Jr.
U. of Illinois Press   Urbana, IL
1988   ISBN 0-252-06020-2

The Cosmos Encoiled
Angelika Gebhart-Sayer
Center for Inter-American Relations
1984   New York, N.Y.

Afro-American Arts Of The Suriname Rain Forest
Sally Price and Richard Price
U. of California Press   Berkeley, CA
1980   ISBN 0-520-04345-6

Amazon Indian Designs
Theodore Menten
Dover Publications   New York, N.Y.
1974   ISBN 0-486-23040-6

Birds And Beasts Of Ancient Latin America
Elizabeth P. Benson
University Press of Florida   Gainesville, FL
1997   ISBN 0-8130-1518-9

*To Weave And To Sing: Art, Symbol, and Narrative In The
          South American Rain Forest*
David M. Guss
U. of California Press   Berkeley, CA
1989   ISBN 0-520-07-185-9

Country Topics For Craft Projects - Mexico
Anita Ganeri and Rachel Wright
Franklin Watts   New York, N.Y.
1994   ISBN 0-531-14316-3

National Geographic Society Publications
Masterworks Of Art Reveal A Remarkable Pre-Inca World
National Geographic Magazine
June 1990   Pages: 17-33

The Moche Of Ancient Peru
National Geographic Magazine
June 1990   Pages: 34-49

Shrunken Head Buyers Beware!
National Geographic Magazine
August 1992   Geographica

Organizations
Global Exchange
2141 Mission Street
202
San Francisco, CA 94110
Phone: (415)-255-7296

Pueblo To People
2105 Silber Road
Suite 101-88
Houston, TX 77055
Phone: (713)-956-1172

Peoples, Tribes and Nations
5703 Ridgefield Road
Suite 203
Bethesda, MD 20816-1250
Phone: (301)-229-8983

Potters For Peace
2216 Race Street
Denver, CO 80205
e-mail: potpaz@igc.apc.org
web site: www.cc.cc.ca.us/pfp/index/htm

Music and Dance
Feel the beat!

Rationale

Music and dancing are integral parts of the lives of most Latin Americans. Music plays a much greater part in socializing than it does in the United States. Latinos, in general, appear to be much less self-conscious about dancing and singing. Two of the most popular categories of Latin music that are listened to and danced to worldwide today are merengue and salsa. Several others form the cornerstone of the traditional dances taught for ballroom situations, such as the rumba, tango, and cha cha. Additional types of music and dance found in various regions of South America include the samba, cumbia, vallenato, lambada, and huayno music from the Andes.

This learning station can be one of the most enjoyable of the entire center. It is not intended to teach the users how to dance or to make them Latin music experts. Its main purpose is to give the non-Hispanic students a taste of the wide variety of music that originates from Latin America, which they might not normally listen to or play on their own. It may also provide the Hispanic students with an opportunity to act as local 'experts' on the subject and help out their classmates. A fiesta held on the last day of this unit could feature Latin music and dancing or even a live band composed of students.

Prior-Knowledge Questions

1. Name any categories of Latin music and/or dance.
2. Aside from the language difference, what do you think makes Latin American music different from North American music?
3. Can you name any Latin American singers or performing artists?
4. Do you think musicians in South America use any instruments that are not commonly used in the United States? Can you name any?
5. Have you ever heard of the 'macarena'? What is it?
6. Do you think Latin Americans are better dancers than North Americans? If yes, why?
7. Do you have to be able to understand the words to enjoy a song?
8. Does liking the beat of a song make you want to understand it?

Answers To Prior-Knowledge Questions

1. Merengue, salsa, cumbia, tango, cha cha, rumba, bolero, samba, lambada, etc.
3. Gloria Estefan (Cuba), Reuben Blades (Panama), Juan Luís Guerra (Dominican Republic), Tito Puente (Puerto Rico), Celia Cruz (Cuba), José Luís Rodriguez (Venezuela), Andres Segovia (Spain), Thalía (Mexico), Alejandro Fernandez (Mexico), to name a few.
5. The macarena is a popular line dance that originated in Latin America.

Objectives

1. Students will be able to recognize at least three of the major types of music originating from Latin America.
2. Students will be able to name at least three Latin American performing artists or groups, each from a different country.
3. Students will be able to name and describe at least one musical instrument commonly associated with Latin American bands.
4. Students will learn and be able to demonstrate the steps to at least one Latin dance.

Assessment

1. Name three Latin music/dance categories. How do you recognize them when listening to music?
3. Name three Latin American singers and/or musical groups, each of which comes from a different Latin American country.
4. Name and describe a musical instrument that originated in South America, Africa, or the Caribbean that is usually used in Latin bands.
5. Which of the Latin music/dance categories is your favorite? Why?
6. Demonstrate the steps to any one dance. You may do this by telling your instructor or by actually dancing the steps with a partner.

Activities

(Do the following for at least three different music/dance categories.)
1. Select a category and listen to one of the indicated songs. Initially, just try to feel the rhythm and enjoy the music.
2. Do the same thing for a different song from the same category.
3. Read or listen about this category from the information provided.

4. Listen to the two songs again that you listened to previously. Try
    to identify the beat and the rhythm that was discussed in the infor-
    mation you read. Try to pick out key characters of the music that
    will help you to recognize it.

Music and Dance Categories

Tango
Album: *Baila, Baila, Baila*
Song: El Choclo

Singers: Sergio Sanchez Tango Kings
Album: *Tango Dance Party*
Songs: entire tape

Cha Cha Cha
Singers: Tropicana Club
Album: *Tropical Vol. 1*
Songs: Medley starting with Bodeguero

Album: *Baila, Baila, Baila*
Song: Frenesí

Singer: Franco
Album: *Mucho Más*
Song: Bonito Y Sabroso

Album: *Exitos Del Cha Cha Cha*
Songs: entire tape

Bolero
Album: *Baila, Baila, Baila*
Song: Perfidia

Album: *La Esencia Del Bolero*
Songs: entire tape

Merengue

Singers: Juan Luís Guerra and 4.40
Album: *Bachata Rosa*
Songs: La Bilirrubina, Acompáñame Civil, Rosalía

Singers: Tropicana Club
Album: *Tropical. Vol. 1*
Songs: Medley starting with Palo Bonito

Singer: José Luís Rodriguez
Album: *El Ultimo Beso*
Song: Amalia Rosa

Singers: The Latin Brothers
Album: *Salsa Y Son Caribe*
Song: Serás Tú

Album: *Baila, Baila, Baila*
Song: El Africano

Album: *Merengue En La Calle Ocho '92*
Songs: entire tape

Rumba

Singers: Juan Luís Guerra and 4.40
Album: *Bachata Rosa*
Songs: Bachata Rosa, Burbujas De Amor, Estrellitas Y Duendes

Album: *Baila, Baila, Baila*
Song: Ya No Te Puedo Querer

Singer: Franco
Album: *Mucho Más*
Song: Andrea

Salsa

Album:	*Baila, Baila, Baila*
Song:	Lamento Boricano

Album:	*Baila, Baila, Baila Vol. 2*
Songs:	Me Hiciste Caer, Amantes De Otro Tiempo, Quédate Un Poco Más

Singers:	Juan Luís Guerra and 4.40
Album:	*Bachata Rosa*
Song:	Carta De Amor

Singers:	Latin Brothers
Album:	*Sucesos*
Song:	El Látigo

Singers:	Johnny Ray Y Salsa Con Clase
Album:	*Los Exitos De Johnny Ray Y Salsa Con Clase*
Song:	Mascarada

Samba

Album:	*Baila, Baila, Baila*
Song:	Brasil

Singer:	Madonna
Album:	*The Immaculate Collection*
Song:	La Isla Bonita

Album:	*Samba & Bossa Nova From Rio*
Songs:	Samba De Una Nota So, Samba Triste

Cumbia
Singers: Tropicana Club
Album: *Tropical Vol. 1*
Songs: Medley starting with Amanecer De Una Cumbia,
                    Medley starting with Festival Guarare,
                    Medley starting with Se Me Perdió La Cadenita

Album: *Baila, Baila, Baila*
Song: La Pollera Colorá

Album: *Baila, Baila, Baila Vol. 2*
Songs: El Siete, Destápate, Abrazaditos

Album: *Nuestros Mejores Cumbias*
Songs: entire tape

Materials
Cassette player/CD player/Walkman, cassettes/CDs of Latin music, headphones, instructional dance videos, VCR, and reference books.

Resources
Books
The Official Guide To Latin Dancing
Allen Dow with Mike Michaelson
Domus Books   Northbrook, IL
1980   ISBN 0-89196-067-8

Dance A While
Jane A. Harris, Anne M. Pittman, and Marlys S. Waller
Macmillan Publishing Co.   New York, N.Y.
1988   ISBN 0-02-350550-8

Music (Cassettes and CDs)

Bachata Rosa
Juan Luís Guerra and 4.40
1990   Karen Publishing Co.
BMG Music   New York, N.Y.

Baila, Baila, Baila
1989   Globo Records USA
BMG Music   New York, N.Y.

Baila, Baila, Baila - Vol. 2
1990   Globo Records USA
BMG Music   New York, N.Y.

El Ultimo Beso
José Luís Rodriguez
CBS Discos Del Peru S.A.
Lima, Peru

Exitos Del Cha Cha Cha
1983   Bertelsmann De Mexico S.A.
BMG Music   New York, N.Y.

La Esencia Del Bolero
1994   Sony Discos, Inc. Miami, FL

Los Exitos De Johnny Ray Y Salsa Con Clase
1994   PolyGram Records

Merengue En La Calle Ocho '92
1992   TH-RODVEN Records
RODVEN DISCOS   Caracas, Venezuela

Mucho Más
Franco
Capitol/EML Latin

Nuestros Mejores Cumbias
1989   BMG Music
New York, N.Y.

Music (Cassettes and CDs) (cont.)

Salsa Y Son Caribe
Latin Brothers
1988   SONOTONE MUSIC CORP.
Discos Fuentes Opa-Locka, FL

Samba & Bossa Nova
1992   Saar sri
Milan, Italy

Sucesos
Latin Brothers
1990   SONOTONE MUSIC CORP.
Discos Fuentes Opa-Locka, FL

Tango Dance Party
1989   M.C.R. Productions (Holland)

The Immaculate Collection
Madonna
1985   Warner Brothers, Inc.
Sire RecordsCo.   New York, N.Y.

Tropical Vol. 1
Tropicana Club
1990   CBS Discos, Inc.
Miami, FL

Note: There is a wide variety of Latin music available due to its increasing popularity and the growing Latin population in the United States. The previous albums are only suggestions based on the author's personal experience with the variety of music they contain. If funding is limited, and only two of the above tapes could be purchased, I would suggest the following: *Tropical Vol. 1* and *Baila, Baila, Baila*. Both of these albums have an excellent variety of music categories on each cassette. In addition, they also classify the music according to category on the lists of songs that come with the tapes (reassuring to those not familiar with Latin music). A suggestion for a third tape is the *Bachata Rosa* album, which is fairly recent (1990) and should be easy to obtain.

The best places to purchase Latin music are in geographical areas that have high populations of Latin Americans. If such is not the case where you live, albums can usually be special-ordered through any of the large music store chains.

The Spanish-language television channel Univision has advertised the following club for Latin music:

Club Música Latina
Columbia House
1400 North Fruitridge Avenue
Terre Haute, IN 47811-1130
Phone: (800)-324-4407

A wide selection of cassettes and CDs can also be purchased over the Internet at the sites **Amazon.com** and **barnesandnoble.com** or from the **Rainforest Information Center** website at:

www.rainforestinfo.com

Spanish
Español

Rationale

Nine of the thirteen countries that make up South America have predominantly Spanish-speaking populations (Colombia, Venezuela, Ecuador, Peru, Bolivia, Chile, Argentina, Paraguay, and Uruguay). Seven of these countries have areas with rainforests. This learning station will permit those students taking Spanish as a foreign language to use their knowledge in a different context. Students not taking Spanish will be exposed to a small number of new words and phrases that deal with everyday items, greetings, or courtesy. By requiring the non-Spanish-taking students to learn at least a few common words and phrases, it provides the opportunity for those students who are taking Spanish (or already speak the language) to act as tutors who can help in pronunciation and practice.

Note: STS = Spanish-taking Students, SSS = Spanish-speaking Students, NSTS = Non-Spanish-taking Students

Prior-Knowledge Questions

1. Does the Spanish alphabet have any letters not found in the English alphabet? If yes, what are they?
2. Do you know any Spanish vocabulary? How did you learn it?
3. Do you know how many (approximately) people in the United States speak Spanish? In the world?
4. Can you think of any Spanish words that have become a regular part of the vocabulary in North America? (How about *chili con carne*? Or have you ever had *guacamole* dip?)
5. Do you think its helpful to be able to speak more than one language? If yes, what language would you most like to be able to speak fluently?
6. Do you think the United States should have English as its 'official' language?
7. Do you think English should be the only language used for teaching in schools in the United States?

Answers To Prior-Knowledge Questions
1. Yes. The letters ch, ll, and ñ.
3. Approximately 17,000,000 people speak Spanish in the United States and approximately 400,000,000 speak Spanish in the world.

Objectives
1. NSTS will learn the Spanish alphabet and punctuation marks.
2. NSTS will learn a minimum of Spanish vocabulary and phrases, including numbers (1-10), salutations (good morning, good afternoon, good evening), commonly used phrases (please, thank you, I don't know), and ten vocabulary words of their choice.
3. NSTS will learn the correct pronunciation of Spanish words.
4. STS/SSS will act in the role of tutors to NSTS.
5. STS/SSS will learn new vocabulary related to each of the learning stations (at least ten words for each station).
6. STS/SSS will use new vocabulary in a written format.
7. All students will be able to identify the geographical areas of the United States with the highest Hispanic populations.

Assessment and Activities
1. (All students) How many letters are in the Spanish alphabet? Name two not found in the English alphabet. Identify two punctuation marks used with Spanish letters, but not with English.
2. (NSTS) Write the following in Spanish:
   a. Numbers from one through ten.
   b. Good morning. Good afternoon. Good evening.
   c. Please. Thank you. I don't know.
   d. Ten vocabulary words of your choice, some of which use non-English punctuation marks.
3. (NSTS) Pronounce your ten vocabulary words for your instructor.
4. (STS/SSS) Write down ten words for each of the learning stations that relate to each topic. Translate those words into Spanish.
5. (STS/SSS) Write a one paragraph description in Spanish of each learning station using the ten words from #4.
6. (STS/SSS) Write a short letter to someone your own age that lives in the Amazon region. Tell your Amazonian friend about the winter-related activities that you have done like building a snowman, having a snowball fight, going skiing/ice fishing/ice skating. (Explain in your letter what those activities are you have done.)

7. (STS) Pretend you are a foreign correspondent working for CNN. You have been sent to the rainforest to interview people who live there about rainforest destruction and how it affects their lives. Use all the information you have gained and learned from all of the other learning stations to form a list of intelligent questions. Your partner will play a native farmer of the Amazon and will likewise use the information from the other learning stations to reply with intelligent and believable answers. Present this interview in Spanish live for the teacher, written, or videotaped as if it were a newscast.

9. (STS) Select any of the books or magazines available in Spanish and read it. Give a brief report on what you've read in English, which can be written, presented orally, or videotaped.

10. (STS) Put on a skit in Spanish where children from the United States meet children from South America.

11. Identify the five geographical areas of the United States that have the highest Spanish-speaking populations. Explain this distribution. Why might this distribution change during certain times of the year?

Materials

Spanish textbook, Spanish dictionary, Spanish books for children, Spanish magazines, and Spanish newspapers.

Resources
Books

El Bosque Tropical - Rain Forest   (English & Spanish)
Helen Cowcher   (Juvenile)
Farrar, Straus & Giroux   New York, N.Y.
1996   ISBN 0-374-42043-2

Un Paseo Por El Bosque Lluvioso   (Spanish)
Kristin Joy Pratt   (Juvenile)
DAWN Publications   Nevada City, CA
1993   ISBN 1-883220-02-5

El Gran Capoquero   (Spanish)
Lynne Cherry   (Juvenile)
Libros Viajeros   San Diego, CA
1990   ISBN 0-15-232320-1

Fernando's Gift - El Regalo De Fernando   *(English & Spanish)*
Douglas Keister   (Juvenile)
Sierra Club Books for Children   San Francisco, CA
1998   ISBN 0-87156-927-2

Invisible Hunters - Cazadores Invisibles   *(English & Spanish)*
Harriet Rohmer   (Juvenile)
Children's Book Press   San Francisco, CA
1987   ISBN 0-89239-031-X

Magic Dogs Of The Volcanoes   *(English & Spanish)*
Los Perros Mágicos De Los Volcanes   (Juvenile)
Manlio Argueta and Stacey Ross
Children's Book Press   San Francisco, CA
1990   ISBN 0-89239-064-6

Gorrión Del Metro (Spanish)   (Juvenile)
Leyla Torres
Farrar, Straus, and Giroux   New York, N.Y.
1997   ISBN 0-374-42782-8

Irene, la valiente (Spanish)   (Juvenile)
William Steig
Farrar, Straus, and Giroux   New York, N.Y.
1993   ISBN 0-374-43620-7

Perspectiva / El Puente - World News Monthly in Spanish
Educational News Service
Phone: (800)-600-4494

Selecciones Del Reader's Digest
Reader's Digest Latinoamérica
2655 LeJeune Road, Suite 301
Coral Gables, FL 33134

Editorial Televisa (Popular Magazines In Spanish)
Phone: 261-27-01 (In Mexico City, Mexico)
e-mail: suscripciones@siedi.spin.com.mx

Student Evaluation Questionnaire
For
Learning Center

(Evaluations should be anonymous to encourage sincere and useful answers.)

1. What did you like best about this learning center?
2. What information do you feel is useful to you in everyday life?
3. What changes would you make in this learning center?
4. Did you have trouble understanding anything in this unit? What?
5. What would have made the above easier to understand?
6. What did you like least about this learning center?
7. Which part of the unit was the most fun? Why?
8. Is there anything about South America or the Amazon rainforest that wasn't taught that you would have liked to have learned about?
9. Do you understand now that South American cultures are both similar and different from those in the United States?
10. Did studying South America and the Amazon make you want to take a trip there to see it for yourself?
11. If you answered "yes" to question #10, where would you like to go and why?
12. Please write down any other comments about this unit. The comments can be complaints or anything you wish.

The study of the Amazon rainforest and the continent of South America could involve many different topics and easily take an entire year to complete. However, this learning center was created to give you exposure to just a few interesting themes, some of which will be related directly to other subjects you are currently taking. These themes will hopefully increase your knowledge and appreciation of one of the most complex and important ecological communities in existence, the tropical rainforest. It is not sufficient just to learn about the plants and animals. A true understanding can only come when one is informed about the land and its people as well.

The following topics are each represented as an individual station in this learning center: *Geography, Biodiversity, Economic Botany, Camouflage and Mimicry, Rainforest Destruction, People and Their Languages, Art and Artifacts, Music and Dance,* and *Spanish.* Which stations you select to complete will be up to you and your teacher. Hopefully, you will have the time and the desire to do them all. Have fun!

82

Reproducible Page for *Geography* Station

The continent of South America is composed of thirteen countries, which range in size from the equivalent of Maine (French Guiana) to the equivalent of eight times the size of California and Texas together (Brazil). The people and life forms that populate these countries are incredibly diverse. This diversity appears to be repeated in the geography of the region as well.

The west coast of South America has some of the driest deserts in the world. These areas go decades without getting a drop of water. Yet not far away, on the other side of the Andes Mountains, are some of the wettest areas of the world. The Amazon is the largest continuous area of tropical rainforest still in existence, covering an area about equal to the continental United States. The large variation in latitude (more than 60 degrees) from northern South America to Tierra del Fuego in the south, combines with the changing altitudes caused by the mountain ranges to provide many different geographical and ecological zones. Some of the most interesting geological features of the continent are the isolated mountainous outcroppings called *tepuis* that are found along the border between Venezuela and Brazil. It was one of these *tepuis* that was the setting of Sir Arthur Conan Doyle's fictional story *The Lost World*.

Approximately one third of all the plant and animal species on Earth can be found in the Amazon rainforest. About 90% of all species are found in all the rainforests of the world. The term that scientists use to describe the amount and variety of living organisms in an area is biodiversity. In a hectare (2.5 acres) of forest in the United States, there are usually 5-10 species of trees. In a hectare of Amazonian rainforest there may be as many as 300. The number of butterfly species in all of North America is a little over 700. In Peru alone there are more than 1,400. There are roughly 850 species of breeding birds in North America, while Ecuador contains more than 1,300. Even fish are more diverse, with more than 2,000 species found in the Amazon River Basin compared to only 250 species in the Mississippi River Basin.

Several reasons may explain why we find such high diversity in the Amazon. Scientists believe that the mild seasonality (no freezing winters) and the constant availability of resources have led to more species evolving with less becoming extinct due to climatic reasons. The longer period of evolution these species have undergone has allowed them to become more specialized, so that more species can exist without competing with one another. Finally, the rainforest is a complex three-dimensional environment that provides many physical places to live in.

Reproducible Page for *Biodiversity* Station

84

Reproducible Page for *Economic Botany* Station

The rainforest has been called nature's pharmacy due to the fact that one fourth of all our drugs originated from plants growing there. For many years the only effective treatment for malaria came from the bark of the cinchona tree. In Madagascar, a drug made from the rosy periwinkle has dramatically increased the survival rate in certain types of cancer. More recently in Peru, the cat's claw vine (*uña de gato*) has been exported by the ton due to its beneficial effect on the immune system. Scientists from developed nations have finally learned that the most knowledgeable people about the medicinal properties of rainforest plants are the medicine men or *curanderos* that use them on a daily basis. Specially trained plant scientists (ethnobotanists) live with Indian tribes for years at a time in order to find out what plants they use and how they use them.

In addition to plants of medicinal value, many plants can be harvested as food. Among these are cashews and Brazil nuts. The rainforest fruit camu camu has more vitamin C than citrus. The fruit of guarana is rich in caffeine and even used in some U.S. soft drinks such as Josta. Chocolate is processed from the pods of the cacao tree. Finally, industrial products are found in the rainforest as well, the most historically important being rubber. Although synthetic rubber is available today, natural rubber is still preferred for certain uses such as airplane tires.

In order to survive, many animals have evolved adaptations that fall under the heading of camouflage and mimicry. While this occurs throughout the animal kingdom, many classic examples are found in rainforest insects. Camouflage is the term used when an animal is colored to blend in with its environment. An insect colored exactly to match its background has cryptic coloration. When the pigmentation is blotchy and asymmetrical so that the shape of the organism is difficult to see, it is called disruptive coloration. Sometimes an insect feeds on a plant whose chemicals make it poisonous or bad-tasting to predators. These insects often have bright contrasting colors that are easy to recognize called warning coloration. Stinging wasps and bees often have such colors as well.

In the 1800's, two famous naturalists (Henry Walter Bates and Fritz Müller) worked in the Amazon collecting and studying the insects and other animals. Bates noticed that some butterflies were poisonous and had bright colors, while others were non-poisonous yet had the same color patterns. He proposed that the non-poisonous species mimicked the poisonous models to gain protection (Batesian Mimicry). Müller noticed that many different species of poisonous butterflies had the same colors and patterns. This results in greater survival because predators can learn to avoid one pattern more quickly than many patterns (Müllerian Mimicry).

Reproducible Page for *Rainforest Destruction Station*

One estimate of deforestation is that there are 20 hectares (50 acres) of Amazon rainforest lost every minute. Many causes contribute to this alarming loss of wildlife and natural resources. Almost all of the world's tropical forests occur in undeveloped countries that have few marketable resources. Governments sell the rights to harvest trees to timber companies in order to generate income. Cattle raising has also resulted in the loss of forest. Wealthy land owners have the forest cut and burned to make pasture for their cattle. People who are subsistence farmers greatly affect the world's rainforests. Although they clear only a little bit of land to grow their crops, this is multiplied by millions of people. Practicing 'slash and burn' agriculture, the forest is cleared and burned to release the nutrients in the trees. After a few years however, the soils are depleted and the process must be repeated elsewhere. Each family also needs firewood for cooking fires. In some countries, ownership of land is not recognized unless the land is cleared and 'worked'. Animal trappers and poachers also destroy the forest. Gold miners and petroleum companies have poisoned streams and areas of forest with toxic chemicals. In some cases, remnants of forests are left but they are not big enough to support the animal populations that once lived there. As in the United States, habitat destruction is one of the primary reasons for the loss of species.

In the 13 countries that compose South America there are five major world languages that make up the national languages. These are Portuguese (Brazil), Dutch (Surinam), French (French Guiana), English (Guyana), and Spanish in all the rest. In addition, dozens of Indian dialects are spoken by the many tribes that are scattered throughout this vast continent. The main language spoken in a country offers a direct clue as to what world power successfully colonized it centuries ago. The Guianas are excellent examples, and on older maps you may find that present day Guyana is labeled as British Guiana, while present day Surinam is labeled as Dutch Guiana. French Guiana remains an overseas department of the country of France. The mixture and intermarriage of European colonists and explorers with the native and indigenous peoples gave rise to many racial combinations which are referred to by various terms today. A mestizo is a cross between a European and someone of Indian blood. The term mulatto refers to a cross between a negro and a white or European. As in the United States, the indigenous Indians suffered terribly at the hands of the settlers of their country, and even today endure great racial prejudice. Various words refer to Spanish-speaking people today. Among the most commonly used are Hispanic, Spanish, Latino, and Latin American. An accepted definition for each doesn't exist.

Indigenous cultures throughout the world have learned to obtain from their environment those elements necessary to satisfy their basic needs of food and shelter. In the absence of the tecnological advances of industrialized societies, Amazonian and other Indian tribes have found practical and often ingenious solutions for making their daily lives easier and more pleasant. They are no less efficient in their use of their environment than the Indians of the Great Plains were in their use of the buffalo. Trees provide transportation in the form of dugout canoes. The forest also yields fruits and nuts and game to be eaten. Fruits from the calabash tree are made into water gourds or dippers. Five to six different plants may go into the making of a blowgun, while another plant provides the poison for the darts. Various vines, trees, and leaves are used to fashion a house, lash it together, and make the thatch that serves as a roof. Baskets of all kinds are woven and used as both receptacles and for transporting objects.

Clay is dug from certain areas and made into ceramic pots by stacking series of coils one on top of the other. These coil pots are hardened by open-air firing in simple makeshift kilns. The decorations on some Indian pottery and textiles, such as those produced by the Shipibo, are a direct carryover from body painting. The shrinking of an enemy's head by the Jivaro, although grisly, was an art in itself.

The Hispanic culture is especially rich in music and dance. Many of the classic ballroom dances practiced today in competition have their roots in rhythms and beats that originated in South America, the Caribbean, and Africa. Among these dances are the merengue, the cha cha cha, the rumba, the tango, and the samba. Another more recent addition, the salsa, used Latin beats but originated in New York City with the Puerto Rican population there in the 1960's.

Various regions of South America have music and dances that are indigenous and easily recognizable. The traditional music of the Andes played on instruments including wooden flutes or pan-pipes, drums, and the *charango* (a stringed instrument originally made from an armadillo's shell) have a spirit and energy all their own. This music is called *huayno* and was immortalized by the Simon and Garfunkel recording *El Condor Pasa*. Other more well known and popular Latin music today includes the cumbia from Colombia and the lambada from Brazil.

The increasing Hispanic population in the United States has led to the greater availability of Spanish music from Hispanic recording artists. Some of these more well known artists are: Gloria Estefan (Cuba), Juan Luís Guerra (Dominican Republic), Reuben Blades (Panama), Andres Segovia (Spain), Thalía (Mexico), José Luís Rodriguez (Venezuela), and Alejandro Fernandez (Mexico).

90

The Spanish language uses an alphabet that is very similar to the English alphabet, with a few additional letters and punctuation marks. For example, Spanish also contains the letters *ch*, *ll*, *ñ*, and *rr*. Some vowels when used in various words will carry an accent mark like this *ó* as in *nación*. Sometimes there are punctuation marks borrowed from other languages such as *ü* as in *bilingüe*. Like any language, Spanish takes years to master, but can be quickly learned to the point where basic communication is possible. The following are a few simple phrases, words, and numbers that everyone should learn to complete this station.

one = *uno*, two = *dos*, three = *tres*, four = *cuatro*, five = *cinco*, six = *seis*, seven = *siete*, eight = *ocho*, nine = *nueve*, and ten = *diez*.
good morning = *buenos días*, good afternoon = *buenas tardes*, and good evening or good night = *buenas noches*.
please = *por favor*, thank you = *gracias*, and I don't know = *no sé.*

Reproducible Map of South America

Sample Rationale
(Written to Attract a Student's Attention)

Note: The previous reproducible pages have been provided to make it easy for teachers to have immediate information available for use in creating the various learning stations and topics covered. They have been written more with the idea of providing factual information than to entice the students into selecting that particular station or theme for study. Below is a paragraph using the theme of *Economic Botany* or *Plants for People* as an example of how information can be presented in a manner that secondary students may consider more appealing or thought-provoking. Whether or not a written 'rationale' is used at any of the stations to whet a student's appetite, and/or how it is presented, is entirely up to the teacher and those creating the learning center.

Economic Botany
Plants for People

Plants play a big role in our lives, whether we realize it or not. We use them for food, we use them for medicine, we use them for shelter. Do you know where they come from though? Do you have any idea what they look like before they make it to the shelf of the grocery store or health food store? Do you know that there are tropical rainforest fruits that have 30 times as much Vitamin C as oranges and 10 times as much caffeine as coffee? Or that coca leaves (from which cocaine is made) are still used to make CocaCola?

What we refer to as 'primitive tribes' have been using plants as medicines for thousands of years, and we are only now beginning to see that many of them work! If you would like to know more about how the lives of people and plants have become entwined, read the information and do the activities at the *Plants for People* learning station.

Specialty Book Dealers

Some of the most useful books about South America and the Amazon are out-of-print or obscure and difficult to find. Below is a list of several book dealers that specialize in titles about Latin America, including archaeology, anthropology, and natural history.

Nancy Fagin Books
459 N. Milwaukee Avenue
Chicago, IL 60610
Phone: (312)-829-5252
e-mail: nfagbo@aol.com

Flo Silver Books
8442 Oakwood Court North
Indianapolis, IN 46260
Phone: (317)-255-5118
e-mail: Flosilver@aol.com

South American Explorers Club
126 Indian Creek Road
Ithaca, N.Y. 14850
Phone: (607)-277-0488
e-mail: explorer@samexplo.org

Oceanie-Afrique Noire (OAN)
15 West 39th Street
New York, N.Y. 10018-3806
Phone: (212)-840-8844
e-mail: oan@computer.net

Bibliofind, Inc.
13 Railroad Street
Great Barrington, MA 02130
e-mail: ADMIN@BIBLIOFIND.COM

Many of the books currently in print can be ordered directly from The Rainforest Information Center at the web site:
www.rainforestinfo.com

Slide Sets To Accompany Learning Station Topics

A series of slide sets are available that treat some of the specific topics covered in individual learning stations. Each set of slides consists of twenty (20) duplicate 35mm color transparencies. Each slide has burned into a corner of the image: © **Rainforest Ventures**. The slides may not be duplicated, or used in any commercial application once purchased. There is no mixing and matching of sets.

Rainforest Flora & Fauna: macaw, toucan, tapir, capybara, agouti, monkey, boa, fer-de-lance, bat, dart-poison frog, horned frog, tree frog, piranha, heliconia, swamp cacao flowers, 'hot lips' flowers, forest interior scenic, stilt roots, buttress roots, giant lily pads.

Tropical Crops & Products: bananas on tree, bananas in market, field of rice, rice being harvested, sugar cane, coffee on plant, cacao (chocolate), cashew, Brazil nut pod, mangoes, achiote, cocona, manioc bush, manioc root, Mauritius palm, Mauritius palm fruit, papayas, jute drying, rubber tree, plug of rubber.

Camouflage & Mimicry: cryptic grasshopper, cryptic hawkmoth, walkingstick on leaf, same walkingstick hidden on twig, leaf moth, green leaf mantid, dead leaf mantid, leaf katydid 1, leaf katydid 2, leaf katydid 3, disruptive coloration, fecal mimicry, sexual dimorphism, leaf katydid at rest, same katydid in startle display, warning coloration, lanternfly, Batesian mimicry, 'wasp' katydid, Müllerian mimicry.

Rainforest Destruction: caiman skulls, stuffed macaw, macaw feathers, toucan beak, snake pelt 1, snake pelt 2, ocelot pelt, jaguar paw, jaguar skull, lumbering with chainsaw, removal of logs, logs on riverbank, logs on a barge, cattle 1, cattle 2, small farm, cleared forest, burned forest, Belen slum, clearing of forest along riverbank.

To preview images or order, visit The Rainforest Information Center at:
www.rainforestinfo.com

Teacher and Student Travel
to the
Rainforest

The best way to gain an appreciation for the rainforest and to learn about its wonders is to visit one in person. The logistics might seem daunting at first, but are actually easier than you think. For example, you can reach the Amazon port city of Iquitos, Peru, in four and a half hours on a direct flight from Miami. Other areas in both Central and South America are equally as accessible from the United States. The growth of ecotourism has combined with an increased awareness and concern for the rainforests to lead to a proliferation of facilities that serve both tourists and biologists in tropical forest sites. Programs are also available that combine rainforest visits or courses with exposure to other threatened habitats (such as coral reefs) or educational points of interest (such as archaeological ruins).

Author and educator, Dr. James Castner, leads tours annually to the Peruvian Amazon. Teachers are encouraged to participate and learn from several doctoral-level leaders as well as native guides who work with instructors. A typical program is eight days and includes a variety of excursions and cultural experiences in addition to natural history walks and lectures. Great flexibility can be exercised with respect to time, costs, and focus for specific teacher and student groups. Contact may be made via the following address:

Dr. James L. Castner
P.O. Box 357219
Gainesville, FL   32635
e-mail: JLCASTNER@AOL.COM

You may also visit the web sites at:
www.rainforestventures.com
www.rainforestinfo.com

JASON Foundation for Education

The Mission of the JASON Foundation for Education (JFE) is to excite and engage students in science and technology, and to motivate and provide professional development for their teachers through the use of advanced interactive telecommunications. It was founded to administer the JASON Project, an educational project begun in 1989 by Dr. Robert D. Ballard following his discovery of the wreck of the RMS Titanic. After receiving thousands of letters from children who were excited by his discovery, Dr. Ballard and a team of associates dedicated themselves to developing ways that would enable teachers and students all over the world to take part in global explorations by means of sophisticated interactive telecommunications.

The JASON Foundation for Education enjoys the support and expertise of a unique alliance of public, private and non-profit organizations who are committed to the improvement of science and technical education for all students. JASON expeditions, supported by extensive professional development for teachers and award-winning curricula, feature live, interactive broadcasts from distinctive sites on our planet through advanced technologies in robotics, fiber optics, television production, computer science, mechanical and electrical engineering, and satellite communications.

During March 1999, the JFE is scheduled to conduct live broadcasts from a site in the Amazon rainforest of northeast Peru. Scientists from various biological disciplines will interact with students and discuss their research from their actual research sites. Any teacher or student interested in knowing how they can view these broadcasts, or in more information on the JASON Project and JFE in general, can obtain such information via the address below. The JASON Foundation for Education is a 501(c)(3) non-profit educational organziation.

JASON Foundation for Education
395 Totten Pond Road
Waltham, MA 02451
Phone: (781)-487-9995
e-mail: info@jason.org

Children's Environmental Trust Foundation, International (CET)

This foundation has put together an internationally acclaimed program of environmental education and advocacy centered around bringing middle school, high school, and college students to the rainforest. CET offers week-long programs consisting of diverse rainforest workshops that are given on-site in tropical forest habitats in Amazonian Peru and in Costa Rica. Since 1992, more than 2,100 students, their sponsors, and accompanying adults have experienced one of CET's workshops.

The mission of CET is not only to provide its participants with a superlative academic experience in a spectacular setting from expert instructors, but to expose students to the complex issues of rainforest conservation and destruction. Students are given the rare opportunity to see these issues through the eyes of local people who rely on the forest for food, shelter, and their livelihood. The impact on students can be profound, often resulting in new levels of maturity, life-style changes, and the first steps to careers not previously considered.

Participation in a CET Workshop includes complete curriculum materials (including a project notebook and personal journal), all travel arrangements, fundraising guidelines and assistance, instructor-led workshops held on-site in the rainforests of the Amazon Basin or Costa Rica, program shirts, and attention to the many details necessary for traveling out of the country with a group of minor students. CET also supports and assists project sponsors in presentations to school boards, with the initial project organizational efforts, and provides continued support throughout the project. CET is a non-profit Michigan-registered 501-(c)(3) organization. For additional information, contact:

Children's Environmental Trust Foundation, International
627 Central Avenue East
Zeeland, MI 49464
Phone: (888)-748-9993
e-mail: cethq@iserv.net

Teaching In South America

Various teaching opportunities are available in South and Central America for those willing to live overseas. Certain organizations work closely with American schools in foreign countries to ensure that qualified educators are made available for teaching positions. Listed below are several of these organizations. Two years teaching experience with certification and a B.S. degree are typical minimum requirements for consideration. Most of these organizations hold recruiting 'job fairs' annually at different locations in the United States.

Association of American Schools in South America
AASSA Regional Development Center
14750 NW 77th Court
Suite 210
Miami Lakes, FL 33016
Phone: (305)-821-0345
Web Site: http://www.aassa.com

International Schools Service
Educational Staffing
15 Roszel Road
P.O. Box 5910
Princeton, N.J. 08543
Phone: (609)-452-0990
Web Site: http://www.iss.edu

International Educators Cooperative
212 Alcott Road
East Falmouth, MA 02536
Phone: (508)-540-8173

Search Associates
P.O. Box 636
Dallas, PA 18612
Phone: (717)-696-5400

Teaching In South America

In addition to the private American schools found throughout South and Central America, there are many other teaching opportunities, especially for those willing to use their skills on a volunteer basis. Some of the organizations listed below use the services of educators. The conditions of 'employment' vary greatly and should be confirmed in writing with each individual organization. For those interested in learning more about such opportunities, I recommend the following book: ***The Peace Corps And More***
175 Ways To Work, Study And Travel At Home & Abroad
Medea Benjamin and Miya Rodolfo-Sioson
Global Exchange   San Francisco, CA
Phone: (415)-255-7296

Department of Defense
Office of Dependent Educational Activity
Office of Personnel
4040 North Fairfax Drive, 6th Floor
Arlington, VA 22203
Phone: (703)-696-1352

Peace Corps
Attn: Recruitment Office
U.S. Peace Corps
1900 K Street, N.W. , Suite 5400
Washington, D.C. 22209
Phone: (800)-424-8580 ext. 293

Institute of International Education
809 United Nations Plaza
New York, N.Y. 10017
Phone: (212)-883-8200

The International Educator (TIE)
P.O. Box 512
Cummaquid, MA 02637
Phone: (508)-362-1414

About The Author

Dr. Jim Castner is a tropical biologist-photographer-writer who has traveled throughout South and Central America during the past twenty years. He has worked as a Scientific Photographer for a major university and is currently an Adjunct Professor in the Biology Department at Pittsburg State University in Pittsburg, Kansas. He has conducted research on the insect fauna of the Amazon Basin of Peru for over a decade with support from Earthwatch, often utilizing the services of many teacher volunteers.

Dr. Castner's photographs have appeared in a variety of books and magazines, including almost every college-level biology textbook. His favorite topics are related to the rainforest and the insect world. Some of his writing and photo credits include: *National Geographic, Natural History, International Wildlife, GEO, GeoMundo, National Geographic World, Ranger Rick,* and *Kids Discover.* His book credits include: *Rainforests, A Field Guide To Medicinal And Useful Plants Of The Upper Amazon,* and a *Photographic Guide To Forensic Insects.* Dr. Castner is currently working on a series of children's books on the flora, fauna, and people of the rainforest.

In 1997, Dr. Castner left his academic position to pursue writing and the development of educational materials full-time. He has been actively involved as an educator of secondary school students for many years, often acting as a workshop leader or instructor of field courses. He designs and leads natural history tours for teachers, students, and naturalists to the Amazon Basin with the company Rainforest Ventures. He often serves as a consultant in many capacities. Dr. Castner is the owner of the *Information Center Web Ring* which currently consists of the following web sites:

Rainforest Information Center: **www.rainforestinfo.com**
Insect Information Center: **www.insectinfo.com**
Medicinal Plants Information Center:
     www.medicinalplantinfo.com
Biological Photography And Consulting:
     www.biologicalphotography.com